Blacker's Art of Fly Making, &c.,

Comprising Angling, & Dyeing of colours, with engravings of salmon & trout flies.

by William Blacker

Please note that the text uses varied hyphenation, such as "fly making" and "fly-making". This has been retained as have been some archaic spellings, such as "scissars".

© 2012 Benediction Classics, Oxford.

ENTERED AT STATIONERS' HALL.

LONDON:
PRINTED BY GEO. NICHOLS, EARL'S COURT,
LEICESTER SQUARE.

PATRONIZED BY H.R.H. PRINCE ALBERT.

BLACKER'S,
ART OF FLY MAKING, &c,

COMPRISING ANGLING,

& DYEING OF COLOURS.

WITH ENGRAVINGS

OF SALMON & TROUT FLIES

SHEWING THE PROCESS

OF THE GENTLE CRAFT

AS TAUGHT IN

THE PAGES.

WITH DESCRIPTIONS OF

FLIES FOR THE SEASON

OF THE YEAR

AS THEY COME OUT

ON THE WATER.

REWRITTEN & REVISED

BY THE AUTHOR

BLACKER, HIMSELF,

FISHING TACKLE MAKER

OF 54, DEAN ST, SOHO,

LONDON.

1855.

PREFACE.

I know not how to apologise for submitting a Second Edition of this little Book to the notice of the Angling few, after the appearance of so many by clever writers, except the many calls I had for it, and a sincere desire of improving farther upon a craft that has not hitherto been clearly promulgated by a real practitioner; consequently my great object is to benefit and amuse my readers, by giving them something practical, which at the present time may be particularly wanted by those who love to make their own flies, whose wants, without doubt, will be found sufficiently supplied in this book; the tyro will appreciate it as valuable to him, and the senior angler who may, perchance, be in possession of it, and who may be singularly fond of making his flies, and amusing himself dyeing the hackles and colours, &c., will, I am persuaded, consider it a treasure.

My endeavours have been unceasing for many years past, in striving to please the great Salmon Fishers and Trout Fishers of this Country, and I must confess that my labours have not been in vain; they have generously conferred upon me their very kind patronage and good will, benefits for which I hold them in very great estimation. Under these circumstances, I have taken much pains to write the book in a befitting manner to suit their tastes and purposes, although my inability in many instances has been an obstacle, nevertheless with all my faults I claim the title of Fisherman, an humble and unimportuned name which no reasonable dispensation can deprive me of.

From my boyhood, I took great delight in ranging along the banks of the beautiful and romantic streams of my native land, Ireland; and having also been for many years a skilful Fly Fisher of no little commendation, in both Great Britain and Hibernia, it is my desire to impart to the world, plainly and easily, the knowledge I have acquired, that all those who wish to become masters of the art, may, by patience and practice, and a close adherence to the instructions I shall lay down, derive the fullest benefit from my experience.

I have endeavoured in the following treatise on Fly-making, to divest the subject, as far as possible, of all technicalities and superfluities; at the same time, I have entered into such full details in the construction of the Fly, that by adopting the process I have pointed out, and following the instructions I have given, the aspirants to the art of Fly-making may speedily become proficients.

In this little book there will be found nothing imaginary, but it is purely written from the practice of angling, so that I may without scruple, justly entitle it The Art of Fly-making, Angling, and Dyeing of Colours. It is also interspersed with many useful remarks that will no doubt agreeably entertain my readers.

No man has taken such pains to improve upon the angler's craft as I; on every article in the whole range of fishing tackle I have made some improvement on rods, flies, lines, reels, and tackle of every sort; and in these pages have left a lasting memorial of my handicraft to the fly-fisher, from whom I have hidden nothing that might retard him in his progress, and who will appreciate it for the great deal of matter propounded in little compass to prevent incumbrance; that the lovers of fly fishing, which has superior claims, may have an opportunity of keeping it in their side pocket,—to be convenient and handy when on their piscatory excursions, the exercise and variety of which will be found advantageous to the health, and the calming of the mind—things not to be purchased; enjoying at the same time the harmonious notes of the warblers of the grove, and musing upon the diversity of the prospects around, while straying along the beautiful streams and vallies of this delightful country.

The list of flies I have given, will be found very valuable, and the tyro will take great delight in imitating these flies necessary for use, and suiting the colours exactly to each, keeping to their symmetrical forms as they appear with his light materials. This beautiful branch of fly-making, peculiarly my own, cannot fail to perfect the angler who is scientific and ingenious, the result of which will be never-failing success.

I have added to the art of fly-making full instructions, and the most approved receipts for dyeing mohair, pighair, feathers, and other materials most useful and appropriate for imitating the natural flies and stuffs the most killing for Trout and Salmon; and which will retain their brilliancy through all the vicissitudes to which they may be exposed.

To bring the Engravings of the flies to the greatest perfection, I have stood at the elbow of the artist who executed this part of the work, that they might be turned out exact to my own models, which renders them and the descriptions more intelligible, as the shade in the fibre of each feather is shown in the plate, in the clearest and finest manner imaginable, that it may be properly seen how these artificial flies are constructed,—the resemblance of those beautiful ones, the productions of the Great Author of Nature, that Trout and Salmon do love to feed upon.

I have also given the principal rivers of England, Ireland, Scotland, and Wales, with the flies best adapted to each, which will enable the fisher to have all things in readiness on his arrival at their localities, and sally out on the finny tribe fearless of disappointment; and for the younger branch of anglers, I have shown the various sorts of fish, with the tackle and baits best adapted to catch them.

The catechism of fly making which I have introduced will be found very curious and instructive to the young beginner, and will afford him every opportunity of retaining the whole process, that when rehearsed in the mind, and perfectly understood, he may apply, with more certain facility, the hand to both material and hook.

Published by the Author, WILLIAM BLACKER,
At 54, Dean Street, Soho, 1855.

An Extract of a Review of William Blacker's Art of Fly Making, &c. &c. &c., taken from "Bell's Life in London," April 8th, 1855.

"The Art of Fly Making, Angling & Dyeing of Colours. By W. Blacker,—Mr. Blacker has been a celebrated trout and salmon angler from early boyhood, and he is known to be the best maker of trout and salmon flies alive. We have never seen such flies as his, for naturalness of shape, appropriateness of colour and for beauty and solidity of finish. In making flies he has "caught a grace beyond the reach of art," and this he exhibits in the *Sanspareil* work before us. It contains no fewer than seventeen engravings on steel and copper, of trout and salmon flies, in every stage of fabrication, from the whipping of hook and gut together to the finishing of the head. These engravings, every plate crowded with figures, are executed after his own models and under his own *Surveillance*, and carefully and beautifully coloured, he standing, as he says, "by the artist's elbow." They contain coloured representations of hackles, wing-feathers, fur, silk, tinsel, in their natural state, and prepared for forming the artificial insect. His profusely illustrated instructions for making salmon-flies are entirely original there being nothing at all like them in any work extant, and he must be a dull scholar indeed, who shall not, after brief study of them, become his own salmon fly dresser. Mr. Blacker withholds no secret and spares no pains in developing by the aid of pen and pencil his own method, and we consider it the best, of making artificial flies for every variety of trout and salmon. He gives numerous, well-tried recipes for dying feathers and all other materials, the colours necessary for the successful operations of the fly-maker. He points out how rods are best made, the best sort of winches, lines and hooks, and proves himself a safe guide to the purchaser. He teaches how the rod, and line and flies, are to be used—the art of casting with them, how a river is to be fished, and how a fish, whether trout or salmon, is to be struck, hooked and landed. He describes the best trout and salmon rivers in the empire, the right season for fishing them, and gives an illustrated list of the flies, stating the materials of what they are to be made, that kill best on them. On flies, favourites of his from experience, he dwells with pleased and pleasing minuteness, and for the first time discloses how the "winged larva," a deadly invention of his own, is to be constructed. Never, was a book more honestly and conscientiously written. It glows with deep-felt enthusiasm for his art, and with a generous desire of revealing everything that pertains to the perfect acquisition of it in all its branches. It is a work of great labour and long pains-taking, unique at all points, and no one could have written it but a practical angler of long, passionate, and devoted experience in the capture of salmon and salmonidæ, and of *ne plus ultra* perfection in the art of making artificial flies, and concomitant fishing tackle. The work is published by himself, at 54, Dean Street, Soho, and we recommend it more earnestly than we have ever done any other work of the sort."

An Extract from "Bell's Life," April 29th, 1855.

"I shall copy a few of Mr. Blacker's patterns as given in his recently-published and very valuable work, entitled *Art of Fly Making, &c*. He is by far the best flymaker I have ever known, and his opinions on flies and fly-fishing deserve the attention of us all. In the book just named he says of the Yellow Sally:—'This is the forerunner of the green drake or May-fly. The trout take this little fly freely if made after this description:—

"Body, buff-coloured fur and a small yellow hackle for legs round the head; wings of the buff-coloured feather inside the wing of the thrush. Hook, 13."

"Several ways of imitating the May-fly. First, Blacker's, as given in his Art of Fly Making:—The body of this beautiful fly is made of yellow green mohair, the colour of a gosling newly hatched, and ribbed with yellow-brown silk, a shade of light brown mohair at the tail, and a tuft of the same at the shoulder, picked out between the hackle, the whisks of the tail three black hairs, three-quarters of an inch long; the hackle to be dyed a greenish buff (dye, according to my recipe, a silver dun hackle with bars across it, called a cuckoo,) or a light ginger hackle bordering on yellow. The wings, which should be made full, and to stand upright, are made of mallard's feathers dyed of a greenish buff, or yellowish shade; a brown head of peacock harl tied neatly above the wings on a No. 6 hook. The wings may be made of the tops of two large dyed mallard's feathers, with fibres stripped off at the butts of the stems, tied back to back. These feathers stand up well and appear very naturally in the water. Large-sized ones kill well in lakes, with bright yellow mohair bodies ribbed with gold twist.

"Second way, from A Handbook of Angling.—Body, bright yellow mohair, or floss silk, ribbed sparingly with light bronze peacock harl; wings, mottled feather of the mallard dyed a pale yellow green. They are to stand nearly erect, and to be slightly divided. Legs, a couple of turns of a red-ginger hackle; tail, three hairs from the rabbit's whisker. Hook, 5, 6, and 7.—Another way: Body, yellow-brown mohair; wings, mallard's feather dyed yellow, and black head; legs, yellowish hackle; tail and hooks as before. During the season of the May-fly, should the weather be gloomy, with a strong warm wind, I would angle with three flies on the casting-line of different sizes, and of colours slightly differing, buff, yellow, and yellow-green, and one of them made buzz. The largest fly should be used as the stretcher; the smallest the upper bob."

An Extract from "Bell's Life," April 1st, 1855 "The Ondine" in the Book of the Salmon, by "Ephemera,"

"Gold tip; tail, small, brilliant topping, light blue tag; body, blue peacock harl, closely ribbed with fine gold twist; two joints of green trogan feather, and one of red orange hackle under the wings, and over their butts blue jay; wings, a careful mixture of fibres of bustard, silver pheasant, yellow and blue macaw teal, guinea-hen and golden pheasant tail and neck-feathers, surmounted by a topping; feelers, blue and yellow macaw, and bright peacock harl, head. Hook, No. 7 and 8. This water-witch, sculptured originally by Blacker, is properly called "Ondine." The first time I saw it I nearly lost my senses, and was upon the point of becoming its victim.

"The May-fly and Phelim Rhu are best made by Blacker, of Dean Street, Soho; Phelim is one of his many good inventions. Dressed on the smallest sized grilse hook, it will on dark days and evenings, and in full water kill sea trout and large common trout in every locality. See a celebrated claret fly plate No. 4, page 108."

Prince Albert's Letter to the Author, enclosing £10.

Nearly eleven years have rolled by, since I sent a copy of the first edition of this work to His Royal Highness Prince Albert, who conferred upon me much honor by a favourable reply to it, at that time I took great pains to illustrate it with specimens of the most costly and beautifully executed salmon and trout flies imaginable, many of which were worth a guinea a piece. In this new edition for 1855 I have given numerous copperplates of these excellent killing flies superbly painted to suit the rivers of Ireland, Scotland, England, and Wales; such choice specimens are they that I think salmon and trout will not refuse them in any river in Britain, they are models of gracefulness, and will prove very attractive to the finny tribe, they are all general favourite flies of mine, and of the great salmon and trout fly fishers of the present day. The angler should never fail to try them wherever he roamed in rivers known or unknown to him, and succesful experience has given me an opportunity of recommending them with the greatest confidence, they have killed fish when they have been half gnawed away, and as a fisherman I look upon them with admiration although they are the work of my own fingers, I think I will not say amiss if I predestinate that the real enthusiastic fly fishers, nine out of ten, will be in love with them.

THE LETTER.
"Buckingham Palace, May 7th, 1844.

"Mr. Anson is commanded by His Royal Highness Prince Albert to enclose Mr. Blacker a cheque for ten pounds for the Work on Angling which accompanied his letter, the receipt of which he will have the goodness to acknowledge."

Contents

THE ART OF FLY-MAKING,ETC., ETC.,	1
AN EASY METHOD TO MAKE THE TROUT FLY.	3
AN EASY METHOD OF MAKING A PLAIN SALMON FLY.	6
TO MAKE THE TROUT FLY, IN THE BEST AND MOST APPROVED METHOD.	8
TO MAKE THE PALMER, OR DOUBLE-HACKLE FLY.	12
HOW TO MAKE THE SALMON FLY, AS SHOWN IN THE BEAUTIFUL PLATE OF ENGRAVINGS ON SALMON HOOKS.	15
PROCESS OF MAKING THE GAUDY SALMON FLY.	19
TO MAKE THE WINGED LARVA.	25
A CATECHISM OF FLY-MAKING,	28
THE TROUT FLIES FOR THE SEASON.	34
FLIES FOR MARCH.	36
FLIES FOR APRIL.	37
FLIES FOR MAY.	40
FLIES FOR JUNE.	42
FLIES FOR JULY.	44
FLIES FOR AUGUST.	46
FISHING RODS AND FLY FISHING.	48
FLY-FISHING FOR SALMON.	52
AN ACCOUNT OF THE SALMON, AND ITS VARIETIES.	55
THE SALMON FRY.	57
A DESCRIPTION OF THE FIFTEEN SALMON FLIES ENGRAVED IN THE PLATES.	60
SPRING FLIES.	68
SALMON RIVERS.	69
THE RIVER TWEED.	70
THE RIVER SHANNON.	71
THE LAKES OF CLARE.	72
THE LAKES OF KILLARNEY.	73
LOUGH CURRAN, WATERVILLE.	76
CONNAMARA AND BALLYNAHINCH.	79
BALLYNA.	81

BALLYSHANNON.	83
THE RIVERS BUSH AND BANN.	85
THE RIVER BANN.	88
LAKES OF WESTMEATH.	92
THE RIVER LEE, AT CORK,	95
SALMON RIVERS OF SCOTLAND.	95
THE RIVER TAY.	96
THE DEE AND DON.	98
THE RIVER SPEY.	99
THE FINDHORN	100
RIVERS AND LAKES ADJACENT TO FORT WILLIAM, ON THE CALEDONIAN CANAL.	101
SALMON FLIES FOR FORT WILLIAM, &c.	103
SALMON FLIES FOR THE NESS.	104
THE RIVER SHIN.	105
THE RIVER THURSO.	106
THE RIVER ESK.	108
LOCH LEVEN.	108
THE RIVER ALLAN.	109
LOCH AWE AND RIVER.	111
THE RIVERS IRVINE, GIRVAN, AND STINCHER, IN AYRSHIRE.	113
RIVERS OF WALES.—THE CONWAY.	114
THE RIVER DOVEY.	114
RIVER TIVEY.	115
THE WYE, MONMOUTH.	115
THE RIVER SEVERN.	116
THE TRENT	116
RIVERS OF YORK AND DERBY.	117
THE HODDER.	117
RIVERS OF DERBY.	117
THE RIVERS WANDLE AND COLN.	118
BAIT FISHING.—THE RIVER THAMES.	121
PERCH.	122
BARBEL.	122
PIKE.	124
ROACH.	125
DACE.	126
CARP.	126
CHUB.	126
GUDGEONS AND MINNOWS.	127
BAITS.	128

THE ART OF DYEING FISHING COLOURS,	130
TO DYE YELLOW.	131
TO DYE BROWN.	132
TO DYE A YELLOW BROWN.	132
TO DYE BLUE.	133
TO DYE RED.	133
TO DYE ORANGE.	134
TO DYE PURPLE OR VIOLET.	134
TO DYE CRIMSON.	134
TO DYE SCARLET.	135
CRIMSON RED IN GRAIN.	135
TO DYE GREEN DRAKE, FEATHERS AND FUR.	136
TO DYE CLARET.	136
ANOTHER WAY TO DYE CLARET.	136
TO DYE BLACK.	137
TO DYE GREENS OF VARIOUS SHADES.	137
TO DYE LAVENDER OR SLATE DUN, &c.	138
BLUES.	138
A SILVER GREY.	139
A COFFEE OR CHESNUT.	139
TO DYE OLIVES AND A MIXTURE OF COLOURS.	139
A CONCISE WAY OF DYEING COLOURS.	140
THE MATERIALS NECESSARY FOR ARTIFICIAL FLY MAKING.	143

List of Plates.

Plate   **Page**

1. Blacker Fly-fishing — Frontispiece
2. Titlepage
3. An easy method to make the Trout-fly — 2
4. An easy method of making a Salmon-fly — 5
5. The best method of making a Trout-fly — 8
6. To make the Palmer's — 12
7. How to make the Salmon-fly — 14
8. Process of making the Gaudy Salmon-fly — 18
9. The plate of Feathers — 21
10. To make the Winged Larva — 25
11. Plate of Six Flies Catechism — 29
12. Plate of 15 Trout-flies — 35
13. Plate of 16 Flies — 40
14. Plate of Larvas and Green Drakes — 47
15. Plate of Gaudy Flies, Nos. 1, 2, 3 — 59
16. Plate of three Salmon-flies, Nos. 4, 5, 6 — 62
17. Plate of four Flies, Nos. 7, 8, 9, 10 — 64
18. Large Spring Salmon-fly — 67
19. Plate of 7 Flies and Salmon — 81
20. Plate of Minnow tackle, &c. — 120
21. Plate of Pike tackle, &c. — 123
22. Paternoster and Barbel tackle — 129

THE ART OF FLY-MAKING, ETC., ETC.,

By WILLIAM BLACKER.

To give something that will convey a durable and correct idea of Fly-making, Angling, and Dyeing of Colours to my pupils, is what I aim at, and desire they should understand: for when they are inhaling the fresh breezes on the river's bank, observing with delight the varied tints and delicate forms of the winged insects skimming the surface, and the sportive trout, pitching over and over, taking them down, this is the time, no doubt, when far from the din of a busy town they will thank me for my trouble in directing their attention to the proper shades, which is the most essential of all things in the Art to be considered. The amusement and pleasing recollections of the Fly-fisher, (when studying the various colours and materials necessary for the formation of the artificial fly—those fanciful ones which salmon take so freely, and the imitating, if possible, by the aid of these materials, those beautiful ones in Nature), will be infinitely more pleasing than can be well comprehended by a careless observer of the craft. Many a pleasant hour may be spent, that otherwise would prove tedious, when confined to quarters of an unfavourable day, far from home, looking over your dubbing book and tying a fly. It gives relief to the uneasy mind by calming the disorders that disappointments may have caused, and by cheering the hearts of those who pursue it as a relaxation and enjoyment. The recommendations on Angling are without number, and there is nothing can delight the heart of the fly-fisher so much as to see the fish rise at the flies on the surface of the water, and their beautiful appearance when landed on the bank; this, with the varied scenery which the windings of the river presents to the imagination, as you roam along, are inducements that cannot fail to gratify the admirer of sportive fish and rushing streams.

AN EASY METHOD TO MAKE THE TROUT-FLY.

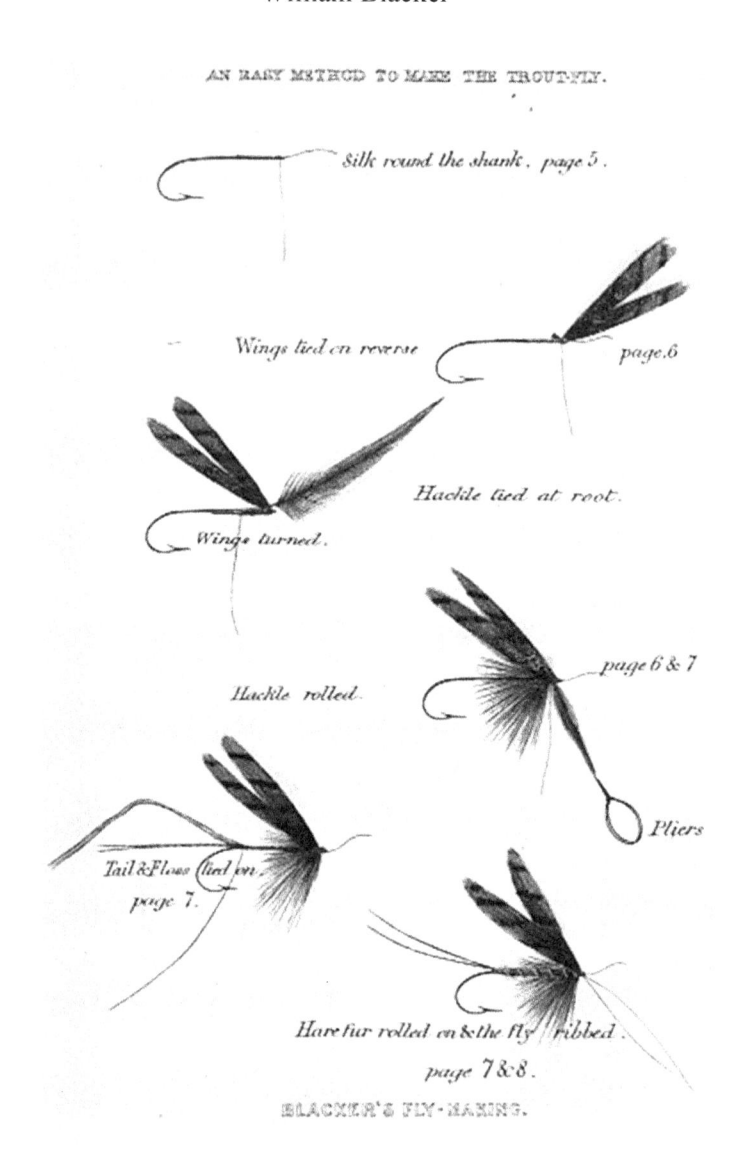

Silk round the shank, page 5.

Wings tied on reverse   *page 6.*

Wings turned.   *Hackle tied at root.*

Hackle rolled.   *page 6 & 7*

Pliers

Tail & Floss tied on page 7.

Hare fur rolled on & the fly ribbed.
page 7 & 8.

BLACKER'S FLY-MAKING.

    I have seen, in days when the fish are not in the humour of taking, a fly tied neatly near the tint, somewhat gaudy, will unquestionably entice them to rise, and will decidedly be more advantageous than fishing without plan. In days when the natural flies are most numerous, the trout will not take the artificial fly so freely; on the contrary, when these insects are rarely to be seen, if the angler can find the colour that is then prevailing, and imitate it, his success will be considerably increased.

In these pages will be found descriptions of Flies that will kill well in every river and lake in the United Kingdom. And those in the "Hand Book of Angling," and the "Book of the Salmon," by the celebrated "Ephemera," will also be found excellent throughout the Kingdom.

AN EASY METHOD TO MAKE THE TROUT FLY.

(*See Plate.*)

The tyro will provide himself with a dubbing book, containing numerous compartments, to hold feathers, furs, pig hair, mohair, hackles, wing feathers, silk, tinsel, scissars, pliers, knife, and every other article necessary for fly-making—all of which may be procured at my Shop, 54, Dean Street, Soho, with Rods, Reels, Lines, Gut, Hooks, Artificial Baits, and every denomination of Fishing Tackle, of the most superior quality in London.

Having laid out your materials on the table, seat yourself by a good light, and proceed as follows:—Take a piece of fine silk, and pin one end of it on your knee, take the other end between your left fore-finger and thumb, and with the right, take a small piece of shoemaker's wax, well tempered, and rub it all over the silk, keeping it tight in your left till it is all covered with the wax, rub it well on the end you are about to tie on the hook with, to keep it firm, for it will be found a very great object to use the wax throughout the making of the fly, as with the working of the tying silk it rubs off with the hand. There is a very beautiful silk of all colours to be had on spools, which ribbons are made of, that works very finely on the hook; when you wax it, take two or three folds of it, and pin it evenly on your knee, as before (or hold it between your teeth and twist it), twist it gently between your fingers a little so that you can wax it well, provide a piece of leather about an inch wide and an inch and a half long, double it, and lay a piece of nicely tempered wax between the folds, flatten it, and when you wax the silk, take the leather between your fingers, open the edge of it, and rub the wax on the tying silk in the same way as before, and you will not break the silk so easily, or dirty your fingers with the wax. You now take the hook by the bend in the left fore-finger and thumb, give two or three turns of the silk round the shank, flatten the end of the gut a little, which keeps it from drawing off, and tie it on underneath about half way down the hook firmly, this done, lay on a little varnish with your pencil. Take a piece of finer silk to make the fly with, and fasten it near the end of the shank, do not bring the silk to the extreme end of the shank to leave room for the wings, as they are apt to slip over on the gut if tied on too near. You strip off two pieces from the woodcock or starling wing, and lay them together evenly at the points, that the wings may be double when tied on (see the Trout-fly wing cut out of the woodcock feather, in the Plate), see that you do not make the wings too long when tying them on, let them be a little longer than the bend; press them tightly with your nails on the hook where you tie them on, and do not clip the ends of the wings with your nails, which gives them an unnatural appearance, but whether you lay them on first, or tie them on the reverse way and turn them back, make a judgment of the proper length; you now tie the wings on the reverse way at the end of the shank, with two or three rolls of the silk, give a running knot over it, and clip off the refuse ends of the roots of the feather; now before you form the body or tie on the hackle, turn the wings up in their place with the thumb nail of the right, and divide them in equal parts with a needle, draw the silk in and out between them, take a turn or two over the roots to keep them firmly in their place, and fasten with a running knot behind them next your left; then tie on the hackle, to suit the size, by the root (the soft flue previously picked off), close to the wings on its back, and give a knot over it, take the hackle by the point in your pliers, and roll it over the shank close under the wings two or three times on its side, keeping the outside of it next the wings, then draw it (the hackle) right through them, let the pliers hang with the point of the hackle in them at the head, and take two turns of the tying silk over it, fasten on the end of the shank which was left a little bare, cut off the silk and hackle points, give another knot or so to secure it before so doing, and lay on a little varnish at the head; now tie on a piece of fine tying silk opposite the barb on the shank, take two fibres of a mallard feather and tie them on about three-eighths of an inch long for tail, to extend over the bend of the hook, and with one knot tie on a piece of fine floss silk about three inches long to rib the fly; mix a little of the hare fur with yellow mohair, and draw a small quantity of it out of the lump with the right hand, take the hook by the bend in your left, lay the silk and hair over the end of the third finger, the hook being held in, twist the silk and hair together and roll it finely to the shoulder, give a running knot or two with the silk close to the hackle, take care to have a little more of the fur next the shoulder to make the body nicely tapered; you may continue to make the body from where you rolled on the hackle first, and fasten at the tail, and roll the hackle over it if the fly is to be of a long description; tail your fly, and tip it with tinsel, and with two running knots finish opposite the barb, at this point before you finish, wax your silk well, and touch with your varnish pencil: if there are any fibres of the hackle or of the wing, or the hair standing in a wrong direction, clip it off with your scissars, and your fly is completed. You may tie on floss silk or peacock's harl for the body the same as the mohair; and you can perceive that you may finish at the tail or at the shoulder, according to fancy—do not lose sight of this plan.

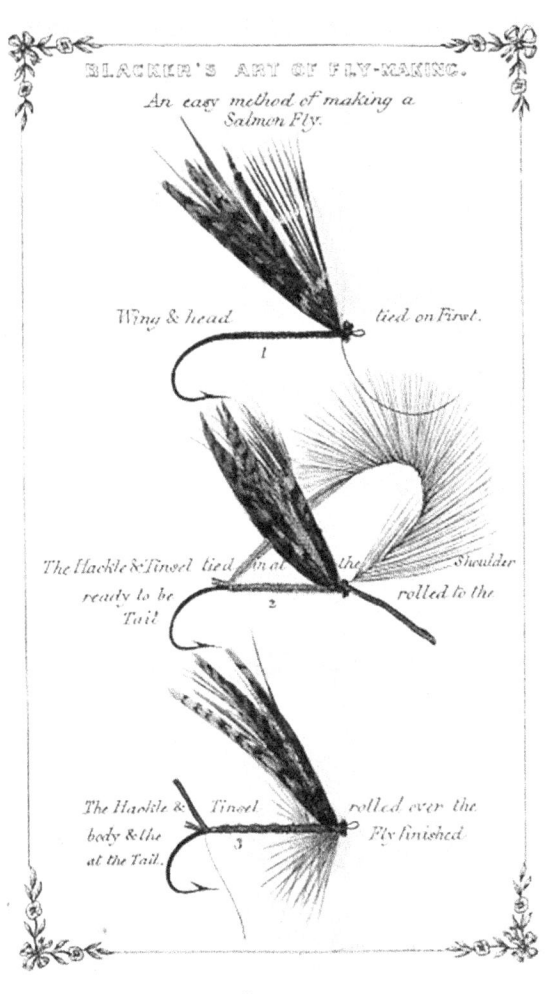

William Blacker

AN EASY METHOD OF MAKING A PLAIN SALMON FLY.

(*See Plate.*)

Tie on the salmon hook to a length of twisted gut or loop (see the gut and hook tied on in the Plate of Salmon Hook, No. 1) firmly with strong marking silk well waxed, and lay on a little varnish; then take two pieces of turkey tail feather of equal size, or mallard feather, according to the colour of the wings you intend to make (see the turkey tail and mallard wings prepared, in the plate of feathers), tie them on the reverse way, a little longer than the bend of the hook where they are turned up (see the wings tied on the reverse way, Plate VII., on Salmon Hooks); these are tied on as the trout fly wings just described, and when turned up appear like the wings of plate No. 1, in an easy method of making a salmon fly—in this plate may be seen every thing necessary in making a plain salmon fly—these flies will be found good killers a great way up rivers from the sea. You hold the hook by the bend, and tie in the hackle at the head of the fly by the root end, and the tinsel to rib it in like manner (see the hackle tied on and the tinsel, Plate II.); about the same place where the hackle is tied on, tie three or four harls of the peacock's tail, twist them round the tying silk, and roll it down to the tail, and fasten with a running knot (see the body of Plate II.) the tying silk is now left hanging at the tail, where may be seen a small portion of the harl left cut, to shew where it was fastened; you roll the tinsel over the body to the same place and tie, three turns of the tinsel is sufficient; you then take the hackle by the end in your right hand, and roll it sideways in rotation with the tinsel, twisting it in your finger and thumb as you turn it over, to keep it slanting from the head, tie it in at the same place with a running knot, and clip off the ends of the hackle; you may tie in a short tail at this place, wax your silk, and finish with two or three running knots, cut off the tying silk, and touch them with a little varnish, to keep them from slipping—press down the hackle between your fingers which slants it to the tail—as the hackle is run over the body from the head to the tail of this fly, it will appear in the formation of the body (Plate III., on Salmon Hooks); when the fly is made with the hackle only struck round the shoulder, take two or three turns of it under the wings, and tie it in there (see Plate III., in an easy method of making a Salmon Fly). The body may be seen in this fly with the tinsel rolled over it, and tied in at the tail; a piece of the harl, tinsel and silk left to shew how it is done. The tinsel and harl are cut off, and with the tying silk, which is seen hanging, tie on a tail of topping, or mohair, feather of macaw, mallard, or any other to suit the taste or colour of the fly; you may tie on an ostrich harl, or peacock's harl, head like Plate I., where the tying silk may be seen hanging: the three flies on this plate, which are correctly engraved, will be found most valuable to the young beginner; and it is an expert method for the salmon fisher, when in a hurry, to make a fly or two for immediate use.

When you wish to mix plain wings without dividing, tie them on first at the end of the shank, and form the head like No. 1 in this plate, which I think is the neatest of any, and suits best in rivers not very full of water. If you notice this plate correctly, it will be seen to correspond with the shape of the natural dragon fly; and as this fly, of various hues, is reared at the bottom of the water, it must be an alluring bait for the salmon and large trout; for when it first leaves the element of its birth, and proceeds to the banks of the river in a very feeble state, directly it receives strength it commences skimming the surface, preying upon the insects flying in the air at this time, and, when it comes weakly out of the water, the fish, no doubt, take it freely.

There is another sort of fly that proceeds from the water, about the size of the flies on this plate, the body of which is of the colour of the blue feathers on the peacock's neck exactly, its legs are a dark brown colour, almost black, hanging long, and few of them; the wings, which stand upright on its back, or I may say, its head and shoulders, for the head and wings at the roots, and legs spring all out of the one lump which is very thick here in comparison to its beautiful slender body of many joints; the wings, I say, are a bronze brown with a moon in all the four like the peacock's tail feather, which in the artificial fly would be just the colour mixed with a little drake feather; there are some of them all brown, and some with bright green bodies, and blue green as above; all these beautiful insects must afford food for the fish. This of course accounts for the artificial representation in use, and it cannot be denied that they take them for natural ones, which the fly-fisher, according to fancy, forms most fantastically, varying on most of the rivers.

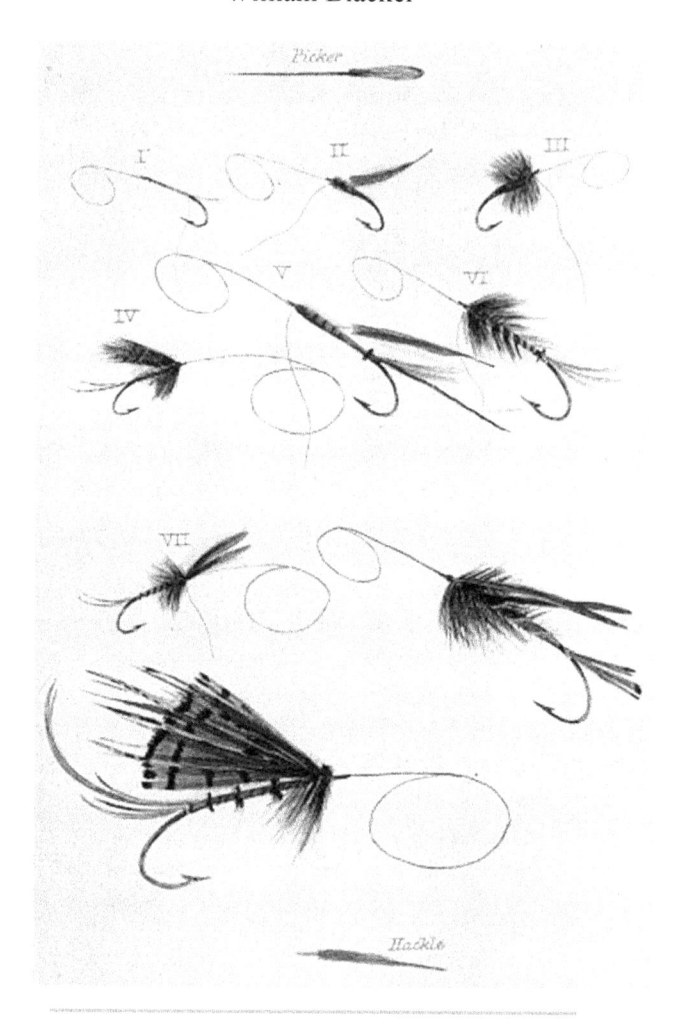

TO MAKE THE TROUT FLY, IN THE BEST AND MOST APPROVED METHOD.

(See Plate with Picker).

The reader will lay out his materials before him on the table, which consist of hook, gut, wings, hackle, feather for tail, body of fur, floss silk, or peacock harl, silk to rib it, wax, tying silk, &c., all things now ready, proceed as follows:—Wax a piece of fine China silk, about a foot in length; if it is spool or ribbon silk, twist two pieces together, and take one end between your teeth, twisting with your fingers and thumbs, not too much; take the other end in the left, and wax it up and down till it is covered with the wax all over; you may pin it on your knee as in the first plan, and wax it; take the hook by the bend in the left hand, say a No. 6 or 7 to begin with, placing your silk just waxed on the shank under your left thumb nail, and give two or three turns of the silk towards you, flatten the end of the gut a little, and tie it on to the hook about half way down the shank, at the same time hold the gut and hook tightly between your nails, and shift it as you go up or down, on the hook shank with the tying silk; the hook firmly tied on, take out one of the wing feathers of the hen pheasant, and cut out of the centre of it two equal pieces to compose the wings, (see the piece cut out for the trout fly wing in the plate of Feathers), you lay these two pieces together even at the points, take them between the nails of the right hand, place them on the end of the shank between the finger and thumb of the left, and give two or three turns of the silk over them tightly, winding the silk towards you, cut off the roots of the feather slantingly with your scissars, as this swells the fly at the shoulder when forming the body; the wings are now tied the reverse way, (see No. 7 Plate, at the sign of the "picker.") The three flies at top of this plate I will explain, when I show how the wings are turned back in their place. You now turn the hook in your fingers and hold it by the head, and of course you roll the tying silk from you; form the tail, body, and hackle, while holding your hook by the shank shift it in your hand till the nails are opposite the barb, where you tie on a tail (see Plate VII) You now draw a little mohair or fur out of the piece lying on the table, and lay it along the tying silk sparingly, twist it round the silk, and roll it up to the shoulder, or nearly so, and give a running knot; take a small hackle and cut it at the point (see hackle at the bottom of this plate), or, instead of cutting it, draw it back a little with the fingers, as you may see the grouse hackle prepared in the plate of feathers, or hackle cut at point in the plate of feathers; tie the hackle on at the centre of the body at the point where it is cut, and give a running knot, and to fill up the space between that and the shoulder, roll on a little more fur, and give a knot with the silk; wax your silk occasionally, as it wears off; you now turn the hook round in the fingers and hold it by the bend; this turning of the hook is the most curious and convenient part of it; the hackle appears standing on the fly, as in Plate II., or V. You take the hackle by the end in your right hand, and roll it up to the shoulder in a slanting direction, giving it an extra turn or two at the head, as you see Plate VII., tie it down, and cut off the stem of the hackle; take the fly between your finger and thumb, keeping the fibres of the hackle under them out of the way while you turn up the wings; you now divide them in two with a needle or "picker," turn up the off side one first and tie it down, then the one next you, and turn the silk in and out between them, to keep them asunder; you then draw all under your finger and thumb, and with the tying silk, give two turns over the ends, which forms a head, and finish on the small bit of hook left at the head, take a turn or two of the silk round the gut to guard it, and take two running knots; the fly now appears as Plate IV., press the fly between the fingers which slants the hackle towards the tail.

As this is a valuable plate of flies to work upon, I will here commence with Numbers 1, 2, 3, and then 5 and 4, these two latter flies are bodies of gaudy sea-trout ones, or grilse flies. The wings are tied on last of the three first flies—you hold the hook by the bend in the left, and tie on the hook, gut, and tail, as you see in Plate I.; you then place on a little mohair to form the body, as in Plate II.; before you reach the shoulder you tie in the hackle, as No. 2, and leave a little of the end of the hook to receive the wings, and let the silk hang at the head; you now take the hackle by the end in your right, and roll it slantingly on its side or partly on its back, placing the third finger of the hand, the fly being held in against the hackle at each roll till you come to the shoulder, take a turn of the silk over it cut off the stem, and give a knot; let the silk hang at the place you are about to tie on the wings, the fly now appears as Plate III., and in this plate you may perceive the right length the hackle ought to be for the size of the hook; you then cut off two pieces from the starling or woodcock wings, and lay them together to make the wings of the fly full, and to appear double when finished, or a piece of mallard feather, like the wings of Plate IV.; you now hold the fly between the fore-finger and thumb nails of the left hand, close to where you see the silk hanging (Plate III.), tie on the off side wing first, holding tight by the nails to keep it on the top of the shank so that it will not turn round with the silk, wax your silk here, keep the middle finger of the left against it while you take up the other wing, and tie it on in like manner on the near side; this plan makes a division in the wings. You must endeavour to keep them tight on the end of the shank, or they will fall over on the gut, but by holding tight with the nails, and drawing tightly with the tying silk, you may soon prevent mistakes, and use every thing sparingly to prevent clumsiness or you will never get on. Now cut off the ends of the wings closely, and finish with a turn or two, and a running knot or two at the very head, and the fly will appear like the finished fly, Plate IV., lay on a little spirit-varnish at the head, which keeps it firm—(this varnish you may procure at the oil and colour warehouses, or at doctor's shops, that which is used for rods is best.)

Now for the two Plates V. and VI.:—

When the hook and gut is neatly tied on, as Plate I., you take a hook, size of the above two, and a hackle to suit; you hold the hook by the bend in the left, and opposite the barb where you see the silk hanging at No. 1, you take a piece of tinsel, tie it on, and give two or three turns just immediately below where you tie in the tail (see the tip of tinsel below the tail, Plate V.), take an ostrich harl and roll it on for tag, which you will see just above the tip of tinsel, then tie on a topping above that, as you may see, then the piece of tinsel to rib the body, which you may see extending longer than the tail; you now take a piece of floss silk, fine, and form the body of it from the tail to the shoulder, as you see the taper body of Plate V., and during the interval tie in the hackle on the centre of the body, at the point where the silk is hanging to receive the wings; take the end of the hackle in your right (first roll the tinsel as the body of Plate VI.) finger and thumb, and roll it slantingly over the body in rotation with the tinsel, as you see in this latter plate, and tie it down at the end of the shank, leave the silk hanging as in this plate, touch it at this place with varnish; you may wing it with turkey or "glede" (kite's) tail feather, mallard, &c., like the plate of the plain fly, opposite No. 7, or like the wing of the gaudy Irish salmon fly immediately under that number at the bottom of the plate, (I mention these two flies in this manner to distinguish them from the plate on Salmon Hooks). These two are models of a plain, and gaudy Irish fly; the delicacy of the body of the gaudy one, as the silk and tinsel is so finely wrought between each joint of harl and hackles, is beyond compare; and the wing is finely mixed, although not so perfect as the beautiful engravings of the twelve salmon flies.

Before I begin the gaudy salmon fly, I will here show how the palmer is made, in two or three ways.

TO MAKE THE PALMER, OR DOUBLE-HACKLE FLY.

You tie on the hook firmly as before, and prepare two hackles for the fly, as you may see in the plate of Feathers, two hackles tied together at the roots, which keeps them on their sides evenly while rolling them on; you hold the hook by the shank in your left hand, tie in the hackles, the inside downwards, that when tied on and finished, the outside of the feathers appears to the eye (see the hackle tied in at the points, and the body and tinsel rolled on, at the bottom of the plates of Trout Flies for the season); tie in the tinsel to the body, and the peacock's harl, or mohair, or floss silk, to form it, at the same place—turn the hook in your fingers, and hold it by the bend; take the harls in your right hand, and roll them up to the head, or mohair, or your floss silk in the same way; take a turn of the tying silk over, with a running knot, clip off the ends of the harl, (leave a little of the end of the shank of the hook bare to finish on, or you will not be enabled to roll the two hackles neatly up to this place). Next, roll the tinsel over the harl, and tie, slope it as you go up; then take hold of the hackles in your right hand, and roll them over the body close beside the tinsel slopingly, taking care at the same time to keep the third or middle finger of the hand the fly is held in tight against them at each turn, and roll them closer as you go up to the shoulder, pull them tight here, and if there are any fibres left on the stem of the hackle that are superfluous, pull them off, still keeping your finger against them, and holding hard the hook; now take a roll or two of the tying silk over them and the knots, give the stem another pull to tighten them, and clip it off, tie down the head neatly with two running knots, and varnish it; press the fly between your fingers to slant the hackles downwards; and if any of the fibres of the hackles stand the wrong way cut them off, although, if they are rolled evenly together on their sides or back, you will turn the fly out correct,—see the beautiful Palmer in the plate, with the hook tied in on the back, which is a perfect model,—these hooks are tied together on the same piece of gut first, and then make the fly over them. It is difficult to perform this job until you know how to make a palmer on a single hook.

The foregoing is my favorite way of making a palmer, but you must be proficient before you can manage it well. I will here show how it can be made in a very easy manner, when you are able to handle the materials, and tie on nicely. When you have the hook and gut neatly tied on, take two hackles, and tie them in at the end of the shank by the roots on their back, tie in the peacock harl and tinsel to rib it at the same place;

holding your hook of course by the bend in the left hand, take hold of the two hackles in your pliers by the points, and when the tinsel and body is rolled on, turn the hackles over the body close with the tinsel on their backs slopingly, till you reach the tail; here let go the pliers, and they will hang with the ends of the hackles still in them, till you take two turns of the silk over them, clip off the ends of the hackles, and tie it neatly with two running knots, lay on a little varnish; the fly will look rather rough in this method when finished, but with a little pain you will soon accomplish it; press down the fibres with your fingers, and cut away the superfluities. You should have a palmer ready made before you always while making this fly, which will facilitate you in your progress.

When you find it difficult to place on the hackles first while you are making a fly, pull off one side of the fibres, and lay two evenly together, and draw them back at the points where you tie them in, as the hackle in the plate of Feathers, and roll them always slopingly over the body to the shoulder, on their edge with the outside of them next the head; and, according as you come up to the end of the shank, roll them closer, which makes the fly appear full there, press them well down with your fingers, (see the three-hackle, or Palmer Flies for Trout, 7, 8, and 9). The hackles of these three flies are beautifully struck.

HOW TO MAKE THE SALMON FLY, AS SHOWN IN THE BEAUTIFUL PLATE OF ENGRAVINGS ON SALMON HOOKS.

Reader, you will have an idea of the sorts of materials you require for the different processes on each hook in the plates, as the models were tied by me in strict proportion, and are most exquisite engravings: You take a piece of twisted gut to form the loop on the fly, double it over a needle, or "picker," to form an eye, and pare off the ends slantingly to lie nice and even when tied, as you may see in Plate I. on Salmon Hooks; wind your waxed silk round the shank of the hook about four or five times, before placing on the gut; hold the hook in the left hand near the end of the shank, lay the gut-loop underneath, and hold on between your finger and thumb tightly, to prevent it turning round when you lap the tying silk over it, and keep shifting your fingers down the shank out of the way of the tying silk in its progress to the tail, which you will see in

Plate I. You now draw out a small piece of yellow, or red mohair, keep it tight between the nails and tie it on, first tip the fly immediately under the tail, as in Plate I.; you make it even with your scissars at the point, as that tail is seen; you now take a piece of yellow or orange floss silk, and lap it from the tail about two-eighths of an inch up to where you see the hackle and tinsel tied in, Plate II.; after having tied the hackle and tinsel on as you see it there, (you may draw the point of the hackle back, as the hackle prepared in the plate of Feathers, instead of cutting it at the point, as you may see also the hackle cut, in the plate of Feathers). You now shift your finger and thumb up the body a little, and just where you finished the knot over the floss silk twist a little pig hair round the tying silk sparingly, and roll it over the shank to the head, or within the eighth of an inch of the head, as you may see in Plate II.; you now take the two pieces of tinsel in the right hand and roll them up slopingly to where the silk is hanging, Plate II., and whip it down; you next take the stem of the hackle in the right hand, and roll it evenly beside the tinsel on its side, or partly on its back (this is done by giving the stem a gentle twist in your fingers) till you bring it to the head where there may be two or three extra rolls of it given to make it full at the shoulder, or where you tie on the wings, (see the hackle, beautifully rolled on from tail to shoulder, Plate III). You now take a piece of mallard feather, stripped off with your nails, and press it small at the end of the roots where it is to be tied on, (see the Mallard Wing prepared in the plate of Feathers); you strip another piece like it, and lay them even together; you take the other two pieces in like manner and do the same, so that each wing, when tied on, will be double; you now take the fly, Plate III., in your hand between the nails close to the shoulder, and wax well the piece of silk that hangs here; you take up one wing and lay it on at the off side, and give two whips of the silk over it tightly, holding on at the shoulder well with the left hand, to keep the wing from turning round under the belly; you now take up the near side wing, and lay it on in like manner, whipping it twice over, and then a running knot, (see the Mallard Wings, tied beautifully on, Plate IV.); and in that plate you see the root ends projecting over the loop, cut them off, and finish it with three or four turns of the silk, and two knots, close to the root of the wings to make all even.

I will now proceed to show how the other three flies are formed—5, 6, and 7.

These may be termed middling gaudy, and are famous for the rivers in the north of Scotland, or the clear waters of Ireland. You perform the operation of tying on the hook as Plate I; tip the fly at the tail, and tie on a topping; take a piece of black ostrich or peacock harl, tie it in at the roots, and roll it evenly over the shank two or three times (see the harl tag, Plate V); tie in the hackle above the ostrich tag, leave it hanging, and roll the twist up the body, previously formed of floss silk nicely tapered (see the Body of Plate V); take the hackle in the right hand, and roll it evenly with the tinsel, and fasten it as Plate VI; leave the silk hanging here to tie on the wings and the head. The wings of Plate VII, may be seen tied on the reverse way, and the body and hackle formed afterwards; they are now ready to turn back in their proper place to hang over the body, this is done by turning them neatly up with the thumb nail of the right hand, and laying them evenly on each side of the fly, with the best side of the feather out. The spots and shades which are perceivable in the wings and hackles of all the engraved specimens of fly, are shown to great perfection—I have described the whole of them, to match the shades exactly, so that it is impossible to go astray when tying on each fibre of feather.

We will now return to Plate VI, and teach how it is to be winged— You cut off a strip from the turkey tail feather, which must be unbroken, as a whole wing; after measuring the proper length of it for the hook, you draw each piece small with the nails where it is to be tied on, as the strip is broader at the root, so that, take it on the whole, it must be narrow where this piece of feather is made small at the roots, as seen in the plate of Feathers, to keep it so whole, touch it with a little varnish, and let it dry a little on the table.

You take hold of the fly in your left hand, close to the head, draw the fibres of the hackle out of the way by placing them under your fingers; take the wing in your right hand and lay it on, catching it between the left finger and thumb on the top of the hook tightly, and give two rolls of the tying silk over it; take up the other wing, like the last, and lay it on the near side, and lap the silk over it in like manner (renew the silk with wax before the wings are tied on); you now may tie on a few fibres of golden pheasant neck, and tail feathers at each side of the wings just put on, and a piece of macaw feather at each side; head it with ostrich, or roll a little pig hair round the silk sparingly, lap it over twice, and finish by giving two running knots over it close to the root of the wings (see the wing of the middling plain Salmon Fly, Plate II, immediately above the Sea-Trout Fly and May Fly.)

The reader will perceive in this plate on salmon hooks, that I have just described a garden, as it were fully cultivated, there is hardly a space left waste, like the broad fields of industrious England, whose sons "never, never shall be slaves." All the other plates are likewise full of useful matter, which will prove my hard labour, and at the same time show that I have hid nothing from the Fly-Fisher in all the processes.

If the fly (Plate V., on salmon hooks) is winged with feathers, like the Irish gaudy wing, prepared in the plate of Feathers, it will be found to approach near the gaudy fly at the bottom of the plate, with "picker" at top.

I will now describe the process of making the Gaudy Salmon Fly, the plate of which is invaluable to the Salmon fisher:—

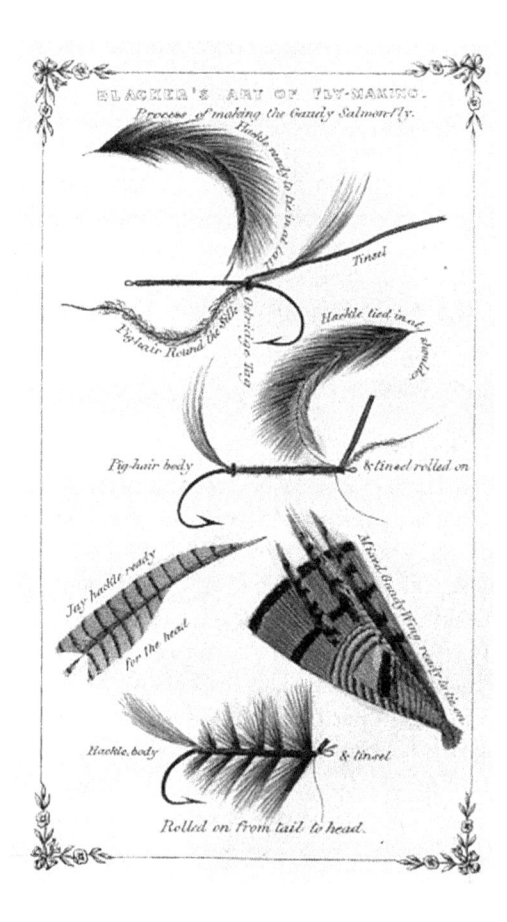

PROCESS OF MAKING THE GAUDY SALMON FLY.

(*See Plate.*)

You commence by tying the hook and gut firmly together, and that it may be more easy and convenient to the reader to accomplish this process of making the Gaudy Salmon Fly, I will tell how it is done in my own favourite way.—Take the hook in the left hand and hold by the shank immediately opposite the barb, here fasten on a piece of fine tying silk, finer than you tied the hook and gut on with, tie on a piece of tinsel, and roll it over the hook three or four times to tip the fly; place the nail of the left thumb on it, and tie with one knot (see the tip on the first fly in the plate, just below the ostrich tag); take a middling size golden pheasant topping, and tie it on just below the ostrich tag with a piece of tinsel, about a finger length, to rib the body (see the tinsel); take a hackle to suit the size of the hook, draw it a little back from the point, that is the fibres (see the hackle ready to tie in at tail in the first fly); take a fibre of ostrich, tie it on, and give two or three rolls of it from you, and as you turn it over keep the soft pile of the feather towards the tail, as this will make the tag appear even, and give a running knot, the less knots the better at this point to prevent clumsiness; now take a piece of pig hair, and twist it round the tying silk (see the pig hair round the silk, and the hackle tied on just above it), roll the pig hair over the body, giving it a turn or two between the ostrich tag and the hackle, that when the hackle is struck it may appear from the centre of the fly to the shoulder; the pig hair is now on, roll the tinsel over it slopingly till you come within the eighth of an inch of the loop; take hold of the end of the hackle in the right hand, and roll it up on its edge, or partly on its back, in rotation with the tinsel, and tie it down with two knots, clip off the end of the hackle and tinsel.

If the fly is to be made with the hackle struck only round the shoulder (see hackle tied in at shoulder, on the second fly in this plate. I have not numbered the three flies on this plate, to distinguish it from the plate of an easy method of making a salmon fly.) See pig hair body and tinsel rolled on; shift your hand up the hook in the left, and hold by the middle, take the hackle in the right, and roll it from you closely round the shoulder, (see hackle tied in at shoulder), leaving at the same time enough of the hook bare at the end of the shank to tie on the wings, and to roll on the jay feather (see jay hackle ready), the hackle supposed to be rolled round the shoulder, cut off the tinsel and pig hair which you see on the piece of silk, leaving another piece attached in the same place to tie on the wings (see the piece of tinsel and pig hair left at the head ready to be cut off, and the silk hanging to tie on the wings—second fly).

The first fly, which we made above, is now no other in appearance than the third fly at the bottom of the plate, which shows hook, body, and tinsel. We now come to the most critical part of tying on the gaudy wings firmly, (see mixed gaudy wing ready to tie on). You take a neck-feather of the golden pheasant with a piece of silver pheasant tail, a piece of peacock wing, a teal feather, and a piece of wood-duck, &c., lay them all evenly together, and break the fibres between your nails, when you tie them on the hook to make the whole small, as you may see done at the root of the wing in the plate; take another golden pheasant neck feather, and prepare it exactly like the last, that the wing may be the same at each side when tied on; you now take hold of the fly in the left, the fibres of the hackle remaining under your finger and thumb, cut away the bit of tinsel and hackle-stem first, take the wing in your right, and lay it on the best side next you, and hold it tight with the left finger and thumb nails; give two laps of the silk over it, press it down tightly with the thumb nail, and take another turn of the silk, place the third finger against it to keep it on, till you lay on the off side wing; take it up as you did the other, and tie it down at the small part of the end, on the off side, hold it tight between the left finger and thumb, pressing it at the same time well down with the thumb nail of the right, take two rolls of the silk firmly over it, hold on manfully with the left, and give it another nail or two with the right thumb, make a running knot, lay it down awhile to rest your fingers; clip off the roots left hanging or projecting at the head closely (be careful always to leave enough of the hook bare to receive the wings, or you cannot manage it easily), now take two or three turns more over the head to make it tighter and even, leaving a little bit of the point to stand out; you then take a strip of macaw, and tie it on each side, clip off the ends, take an ostrich harl and tie it on about the centre of the head, and roll it over from you two or three times, the downy part of the stem next the loop to keep it all the one way, and when up to the root of the wings, take the silk which hangs here lap it twice over, and give a running knot; clip off the silk and end of the harl, lay on a little varnish very lightly at the point, and where the silk has been just tied down, keep the varnish off the ostrich harl; you may take a little pig hair, and twist it round the silk, roll it over the head very sparingly, and finish at the root of the wings in the same manner, laying on a little varnish.

BLACKER'S ART OF FLY-MAKING.

- Grouse Hackle prepared
- Golden Pheasant topping
- Bunch of Hackles prepared for dyeing
- Trout Fly Wing
- Woodcock Wing Feather
- Two Hackles for the Palmer Fly
- Hackle prepared
- Hackle cut at point
- Irish Gaudy Wing prepared
- Mallard Wing prepared for Scotch Fly
- Turkey Wing prepared

I will here repeat the tying on of the gaudy wing, with two or three fibres of various sorts of feathers, &c., which may be a little more easy to accomplish than the foregoing to the young beginner.

When you have the tail, tinsel, and hackle put together on the hook, and the eighth of an inch of the shank left bare to receive the wings; wax the silk well that it may make the head firm, and proceed thus.—First strip off two fibres of the peacock's wing feather, and place them with three or four fibres of brown mallard, and the same quantity of spotted turkey tail, add to it a piece of neck and tail feather of the golden pheasant, with a little guinea hen, teal, and red macaw feather, yellow, orange, and blue. Keep these all even together, and break them at the roots like the gaudy wing in the last plate, and divide them in equal parts; now having mixed both your wings alike, take up one wing in your right forefinger and thumb nails and hold it tightly, take up your fly with the left hand, and with the right hand place the wing on at the off side, laying it under the fore-finger of the left hand, and with the right hand give two turns of the tying silk over it, at the same time holding on tight between the nails of the left hand, and press it down with the thumb nail of the right, which keeps the head firm; then in like manner take up the other wing and place it on the near side, keep the wings the same length, and to extend two eighths of an inch longer than the bend of the hook, having taken two laps over the near side wing, cut off the root ends at the head closely, holding tight with the left-hand nails, and press both wings down tightly with the right thumb nail; wax the silk well here, and lap it over the part where you cut off the ends evenly; bring the silk down on the gut and give three or four rolls of it just below the point of the shank to guard it from friction when throwing the fly; bring the silk up again close to the root of the wings, and tie on a fibre of blue and yellow macaw tail feather for horns, let them be the eighth of an inch longer than the wings, clip off the ends; take a jay feather and prepare it, tie it on at the off side of the head with the bare side next the belly of the fly, roll it with the right hand over the head, about three turns, and lap the silk over it while under the nail of the left; cut off the stem, lay on a blue kingfisher feather each side, tie on a black ostrich harl, give three or four rolls of it over the head, letting the stem be next to the root of the wings as you roll it, take it under the nail of the left thumb, and lap two turns of the silk over it close to the root of the wings, and with the finger and thumb press up the fibres of the ostrich towards the wings, to make it stand even in its proper place; cut off the silk, and lay on a little varnish at the point of the head, and your fly is completed.

As it is my intention to instruct the reader in every point necessary for his benefit, according to my own knowledge and experience, throughout the pages of this book, it affords me much pleasure to be enabled to do so, and to offer something to the fly-fisher worth having, there is scarcely a page he opens that he will not find something valuable to himself, if he is a real lover of the art. "There is a pleasure in angling that no one knows but the angler himself."

I will now show how the India-rubber Green Drake is made, with a cock-tail, like the beautiful engraving in the plate, (see Green Drake). The Grouse, and Golden Plover hackle may also be made in a similar manner, to suit fine evenings in the summer, without the tail.

To compose the fly, take a piece of gold tinsel, and cut a long strip of light india-rubber very thin, hackle, wings, tail, and all laid down ready,—tie the gut on the top of the hook, to project about three-sixteenths of an inch below the bend, or tie the gut underneath in the usual way, and lay a piece of gut on the top somewhat thicker, to work the tail upon, (see the tail in the engraving,—look often at the flies to refresh the memory); take three hairs of the mane of a black horse, and tie them on the end of the piece of gut, about an inch in length, let the silk be fine and well waxed, then tie in the end of the gold tinsel, and the finest end of the piece of india-rubber at the tail, that the thick end may be towards the shoulder to make it taper; after the body is made very even with a little yellow floss silk, hold the fly by the shank in the left hand, with the nails in close contact with each other, and roll the tinsel closely up, shifting your hand; this fastened down with the tying silk, take hold of the india-rubber in the right, and the extreme end of the gut tail in your left nails; warm the rubber a little in the fingers to soften it, draw it out to its full extent, and roll it over the end of the gut, and at every roll keep the third finger of the left hand tight against it to prevent it starting, move the nails up the hook as you proceed with the rubber to the shoulder; give two laps of the tying silk over it, and a running knot. The body now formed, take a very light brown grouse hackle (see the grouse hackle prepared in the plate of Feathers,—the partridge and the plover hackles are prepared in the same way, and all feathers of this shape for the throat, you may either draw them back at the end, or cut them like the wren tail feather), and tie it on at the shoulder, roll it about three times over on its back, keeping the fibres down towards the left under the fingers, tie the stem with a running knot, and do not give too many laps of the tying silk at the head to make it bulky, for it occasions the wings to turn round on the hook, as then there is no foundation for them, but when they are tied hard on the hook, they sit firm—you can not wing it neatly otherwise; to prevent a vacancy at the shoulder, lay on a little yellow-green mohair to fill it up, and roll the hackle over it, you may now guard the gut with the silk before you tie on the wings, do not allow the body of the fly to come too close up to the head, or as I said before, you cannot tie on the wings properly. Now take the dyed mallard feather for the wings, strip two pieces off, and lay them together for one wing, and two pieces for the other wing in like manner; hold the body by the left close to the head, and lay on the off side wing first, hold it tight under the nails of the left, and take a turn or two of the silk tightly over it, take up the other wing and lay it on, catching it under the nails of the left, taking two turns more over it in the same way, and press it tight down with the nails of the right thumb, give another turn or two of the silk, press back the roots of the wings with the thumb nail of the right, cut them close off, roll the silk evenly over it, and give two knots, now take a peacock's harl, tie it in by the root end, and roll it over the head two or three times towards the wing, and tie it firmly here with two knots of the tying silk, cut off silk and harl, lay on a little varnish, and your fly is completed; press up the head to make it look even, cut off all superfluous fibres that may stand uneven, so that all will appear like the plate.

There is another excellent way of making a body:—thus, take a piece or length of very flat gut, and soak it well in hot water till it becomes soft, tie it in at the end of the tail as you did the india-rubber, form a body nicely tapered of straw, roll some white floss silk over it at intervals, roll the soft gut closely over it to the head and tie it fast; then put a small partridge hackle round the throat, and wing it the same as before. Before you lay on the straw, cut it taper to suit the size of hook you are using, gold-beater's skin rolled over flat gold tinsel is also good.

I will here teach the making of the beautiful Winged Larva, specimens of which are shown in the plate with the May Fly. There is nothing can exceed the beauty of these flies, and as artificial specimens for killing fish during easterly winds they are invaluable.

It was in a strong east wind which lasted some weeks, five or six years ago, that I had such great success with this sort of fly in the river Tweed; grilse, sea-trout, and river-trout took it greedily. The two engravings in the plate of these flies are very beautiful. It would be a general killer in heavy running rivers under trees, or in rapid streams.

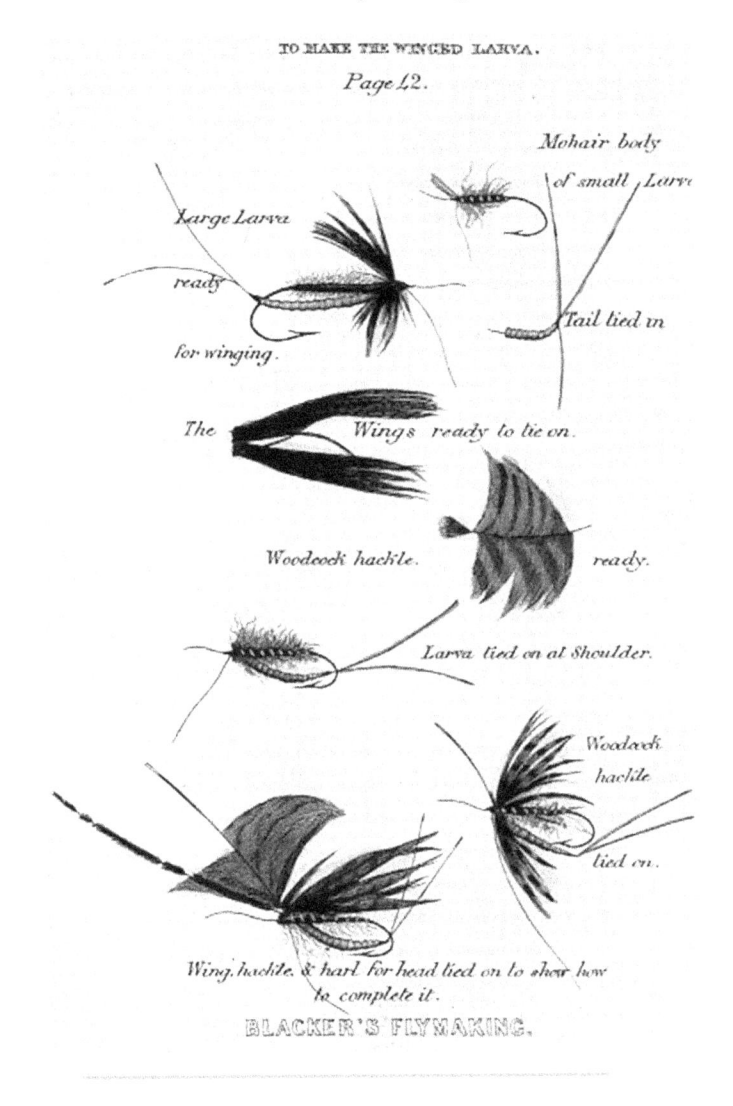

TO MAKE THE WINGED LARVA.

Tie on the hook and gut as before (say a hook about No. 8) and form a brown body of mohair on it, wing the fly with a portion of hen pheasant tail feather and woodcock wing; having the yellow brown body formed on the hook, and the wings ready to tie on, take a piece of the shrivelled larva you will find attached to the ends of the lengths of salmon gut, choose those that are nice and taper, and at the fine end tie on two fibres of golden pheasant neck feather for tail, clip off the end of the gut, lay on a little varnish at the end of the tail to keep it from coming off; now tie on the larva close to the shoulder, cut off the end of the gut, lay on a little varnish there, take some mohair of the same colour as the body, and roll it over the throat to cover the tying, leaving at the same time enough of the hook to receive the wings, you then take a light brown grouse hackle, off the neck of the bird, and roll it twice round the shoulder for the legs, or a woodcock feather, to be found at the root of the wings, outside, the latter I think is best. Now tie the wings on a little longer than the bend of the hook, clip off the ends at the head, and form a head with a piece of peacock harl, of a bronze colour as usual, fasten with the silk, and cut off all the superfluities. It would be well to draw out a little of the mohair at the shoulder to hang over the larva body, and to flatten the end of the gut a little where you tie on the tail, which keeps it on. Tie the larva at the side, so as it may appear like a double body to the fish in the water. It may be made by tying on the wings first, and let them remain until the body, the larva, and the hackle, are all tied in their proper places, and then turn back the wings over the body with your thumb nail, and tie them firmly down with the silk, taking two laps over the roots, and finish with two knots on the end of the shank immediately above the head.

Do not neglect to tie in the larva tightly below the wings at the shoulder, to prevent it drawing out from the mohair body. You must hold on tight and press it well down with the nail of the right thumb, as you do the wings when tying them on last. It is best to look at the larvas engraved in the plate occasionally, to give you an idea how it is done. When the wings are turned up last, and a head formed of the root of them with the tying silk, you next roll on a piece of brown peacock harl at the root of the wings, a harl with long pile or fibres is best, as you can press it up with your fingers to hang over the root of the wings.

The great nicety in making this fly to look well is, in tying on the two fibres of the golden pheasant feathers at the tail with fine silk, and the tying on of the larva itself at the shoulder of the fly, and then covering the silk that appeared bare with a little mohair twisted round the tying silk, and then rolled over it; it is over this bit of mohair the hackle should be rolled, and secured with two knots.

The wing of the small larva in the plate is tied on last, and a most curious and killing looking fly it is; the other one does best in deep water, or for grilse or sea-trout in July and August, particularly in the latter month.

The Salmon Fly, No. 11, in the centre of the plate, with the larvas, is a capital specimen for the light streams north of the Tweed, and would kill well in that splendid river at low water in summer, particularly at the "Throughs," three miles above the town of Kelso.

The above fly I will describe hereafter, with the other engravings in the plates.

To proceed regularly with the various methods of Fly Making, before touching on another subject, will be much more convenient to the tyro as he proceeds, so I will finish this branch of an "Angler's Education" with a Catechism, which will be found instructive and very curious to the beginner. It is accompanied with a copper-plate engraving of six flies, showing the whole process to the eye, which cannot fail to give a lasting idea to the fly maker who will properly study it.

In this last process, the reader should lay out every thing necessary for making a single fly in a piece of folded paper, so that he can look at the various articles as he rehearses them over in the book,—this will keep them more strongly in his mind.

Have each article to suit the size of the hook exactly, that when the fly is completed, it will appear in strict proportion: for instance, the hackle should be chosen small to suit the legs of the trout fly, and the large flies to have hackles off the saddle of the cock, that are old and stiff, to withstand the motion of the water; and fine silk, both floss and tying for the bodies of the small flies, and every thing in unison, as you read in the book; handling every thing sparingly, delicately, and nicely in the fingers. There is a good deal of the "battle fought" by letting the nails grow to a pretty fair length so as to hold on grimly.

A CATECHISM OF FLY-MAKING,

By WILLIAM BLACKER

Question.—What do you mean by Fly-making?

Answer.—I mean the artificial assimilation of those beautiful insects that appear on brooks and rivers during the summer season.

Q.—What are these artificial flies used for in general?

A.—They are principally used to afford gentlemen rural amusement and recreation, by their taking both trout and salmon with the rod, line, and fly.

Q.—Name the different materials requisite for making the Artificial Fly.

A.—The necessary materials for making the Artificial Fly are as follows:—various kinds of feathers, furs, mohair, pig hair, dyed hackles, silks, tinsel, &c., &c.

Q.—When the tyro has all the materials prepared, and seated at the table, how does he commence to make the fly?

A.—First, the hook is firmly tied on the gut, and one eighth of an inch of the end of the shank left bare to receive the wings (see plate, hook, gut, and tail, tied on).

Q.—How are the wings tied on?

A.—They may be tied on the reverse way first, at the extreme end of the shank, and after the tail, body, and legs are formed, turn up the wings, divide and tie them down, and form the head.

BLACKER'S ART OF FLY-MAKING.

To make the Trout Fly as taught in the
CATECHISM.

The Hook — Gut and Tail tied on.

The Tinsel — tied on, & Mohair round the Silk

The Tinsel — rolled on, & Hackle tied at point.

The Hackle — rolled on with the Tinsel.

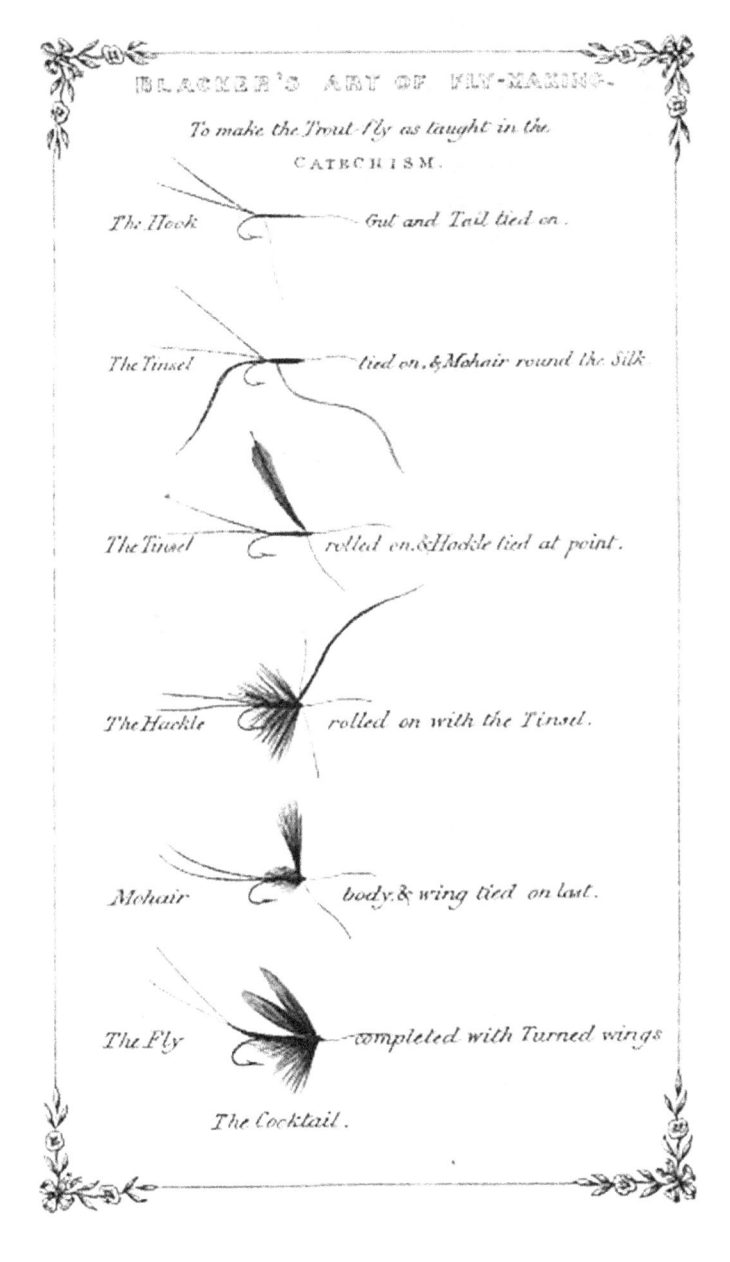

Mohair — body & wing tied on last.

The Fly — completed with Turned wings

The Cocktail.

Q.—Is there any other way of placing on the wings of a trout fly?

A.—Yes, by forming the tail, body, and legs first, and tie on the wings last.

Q.—Having the wings the reverse way, to appear in strict proportion over the fly when turned, what is the next part to be performed?

A.—Next, I take hold of the shank opposite the barb in my left, and here tie on a short piece of tinsel for the tip, roll it over two or three times evenly, and secure it with a running knot, immediately above this tie on the tail.

Q.—When the wings are tied on reversed, the tip and tail secured, how do you form the body?

A.—I take hold of the hook in my left hand close to the tail, and with my right draw out a small quantity of mohair, twist it round the tying silk close to the hook, draw it gradually full under the fingers to taper it, I then roll it closely over the shank to the root of the wings and fasten it. Leave a vacancy to receive the hackle if rolled on at the shoulder.

Q.—If there is not sufficient mohair twisted on the silk to form the whole body, what must be done?

A.—When the mohair on the silk becomes short, I tie it down on the centre of the shank, and tie in the point of the hackle here (see the second and third flies in the plate of this process), and apply a little more stuff to fill the shoulder, leaving a little of the hook to receive the wings.

Q.—Having tied the hackle on towards the shoulder of the fly, how do you strike it in its proper place?

A.—I hold the hook in my left hand by the bend, and with the right take hold of the stem of the hackle and roll it round the shank on its back, and tie it down (the fly may be ribbed and hackled from the tail like the fourth fly in the plate).

Q.—The hackle, body, tail, and tinsel now neatly tied, how do you tie on the wings?

A.—I now hold the fly in my left hand by the body, drawing the fibres underneath my finger and thumb out of the way, lay on the wings double, catch them under the nails of the left and give two laps of the tying silk over them, press them down at this place with the right nail divide and let the fibres of the hackle spring up between them, cut off the roots, lap the silk closely over the head and fasten with two knots (see the cock tail at the bottom of this plate).

Note.—The wings of this fly were tied on first, as seen, and turned up last; the fuller the fly is at the shoulder the more the wings will stand upright on the back, and it often occurs that when the wings of the fly lie flat on the back, and it happens to be an end fly on the casting line, which is usually under the surface of the water, that the fish takes it for a drowned fly eagerly, and the wings much longer than the bend of the hook, this is not unnatural, as the wings of numbers of the brown and olive flies seen on the water have their wings much longer than the body, and when not on the wing lie flat on their backs.

I will here give a more easy way of making a Trout fly.

Q.—How do you commence to make the Fly in this way?

A.—I tie on the wings first, turn them up, tie down the head, and finish the fly at the tail.

Q.—When the wings are tied on first, and turned before you commence the body and legs, how do you proceed?

A.—I take a small hackle to suit the size of the hook, strip off the flue, and tie it on by the root at the head, and a piece of tinsel to rib the body.

Q.—Having tied on the hackle thus, what is the next thing to be done?

A.—I draw out a little mohair, twist it tightly round the tying silk, roll it down to the tail and fasten it, and roll the tinsel over in like manner.

Q.—The body and tinsel being formed, how is the hackle struck on?

A.—I take hold of the hackle in my right hand with either my fingers or pliers, and roll it over the body to the tail, fasten and cut off the ends, tie in a tail and the fly is complete. This is the style of the fifth fly in the plate.

Q.—When a fly is to be made in the above way without wings, called a hackle fly, how is it done?

A.—Having previously tied, I take two hackles of equal size, lay them even together, and tie them on by the roots at the end of the shank, and then the piece of tinsel to rib it.

Q.—How do you form the body and tinsel after tying on the hackles?

A.—I twist a very small quantity of mohair round the silk and roll it to the tail, or a peacock's harl, and fasten it there, over this I roll the tinsel.

Q.—As the hackles are a nice point to perform, how are they struck?

A.—I take hold of the hackles with the pliers at the points, both to stand the one way, give two rolls round the shoulder to make it full, and proceed with them slantingly on their backs to the tail, let the pliers hang with them and roll the tying silk twice over them, cut off the superfluous fibres of the hackles, take two running knots, and lay on a little varnish to harden the tying, press down the hackles with the fingers to slope them towards the tail, and the fly is completed.

Q.—When you wish to make a larger Salmon Fly, how do you undertake it?

A.—I tie on the hook and gut firmly together, as in Plate I, on salmon hooks, take hold of it by the shank opposite the barb, roll on a piece of broad tinsel to tip it, tie on a topping for tail, with a black ostrich tag.

Q.—Having gone thus far, how do you manage the pig hair body?

A.—Having laid before me two or three colours of pig hair, I roll a piece of fine floss silk on first next the tail, I then twist a piece of pig hair on the silk, roll it up towards the head, shifting up a little and tie, take another piece of hair, and another, and do in like manner (see the pig hair body of No. 2, on salmon hooks).

Q.—How is the hackle struck on over the body?

A.-Having held the fly by the shank to form the body, I now turn it and hold it by the bend, the hackle and tinsel previously tied in, as in Plate II, on salmon hooks, I roll the tinsel up first and the hackle next in rotation with it; Plate V. will show the tinsel rolled over the floss silk body, and the hackle ready to roll on.

Q.—Having rolled on the hackle, and turned a jay hackle over the shoulder, how do you proceed with the wing?

A.—I take two golden pheasant neck feathers and tie them on tightly first, then sprig them at each side with various fibres of feathers (see the wing in the plate prepared).

Q.—How do you cover the lump occasioned by the quantity of tying silk at the head?

A.—I draw out a small quantity of pig hair, twist it on the tying silk, and roll it over two or three times towards the root of the wings tightly, give three knots, lay on a little varnish, cut off the silk, and the fly is finished.

Note.—If you make a pike fly, use large double hooks and gymp, with broad tinsel, and make the body full with pig hair, large saddlecock hackles for legs, wing them with peacock moon feathers, and add two large blue beads over spangles for eyes, and green or red pig hair towards the head. Fasten on the beads with fine copper wire, rolling it over the head two or three times, and also three times through the eyes, and tie down the wire tightly with the silk; roll the pig hair round the silk and then over the head and between the beads, fasten it with three knots, and lay on the varnish.

These large artificial flies kill pike or jack best on windy days with rain; they will not rise at the fly on fine days, except there is a strong ripple on the water. You humour the fly on the surface as you would move a salmon one, using a strong rod, reel, and line. If he is a large fish, he will rush off with the fly when hooked; but, if a small one, lift him out when he makes a double quick shake on the top of the water. I would advise the fisher to strike a jack quickly, for he often throws the fly out of his mouth when he finds the deception.

THE TROUT FLIES FOR THE SEASON.

I will now give a description of those flies which will be found most killing, as they are imitations of the natural ones that appear in each month, so that the fly-fisher may practice with them to very great advantage.

The numbers of each correspond with the engravings in the plates of the catalogue of flies.

The Trout is a game and sportive fish, and affords much amusement to the fly-fishers, as well as being generally esteemed the best of our fresh-water fishes for the table. The spawning time of the trout is much the same as that of the salmon, about October and November, and their haunts very similar; they fix upon some gravelly bottom to deposit their spawn, in either river or lake, and are never good when big with roe. After they have spawned they become lean and wasted, and their beautiful spots disappear; in this state they retire to the deep and still parts of the river during the winter months. As soon as the weather becomes open in February, they begin to leave the deeps and approach the rapid streams, where they soon obtain vigour for the summer sport. They delight in sandy and rocky beds and pools, into which sharp and swift streams run, and under shady banks, behind large stones and in eddies; in streams where there are sedges and weeds in the spring of the year. In the summer months they get strange, and haunt the deepest parts of swift running streams; they are found also at the upper ends of mill-pools and weirs, under bridges, and in the return of streams where the water boils in deep places. At the decline of the year they resort to the tails of streams and deep water.

They are in season from February till the end of September.

Blacker's Art of Fly Making, &c.,

These few suggestions may benefit the young angler by giving him an idea of knowing where to cast his flies for them.

FLIES FOR MARCH.

No. 1. The March Brown.—The body is made of light brown mohair, mixed with a little fur of the hare's neck, and a little yellow mohair, ribbed with yellow silk; a small brown partridge hackle for legs (this feather is found on the back of the partridge), hen pheasant wing feather for the wings, and two fibres of the same bird's tail feather for the tail of the fly. No. 8 hook. This fly is well taken by the trout, and continues good till the end of April. The following flies appear before the March brown, but it being a great favorite, I have given it first.

No. 2. The Early Dark Dun.—The body is made of water-rat's fur, mixed with a little red mohair, the red more towards the head, an iron-blue dun hackle for legs, and the wings of water-hen or water-rail wing. No. 9 hook.

There is another variety or two of this fly that kill well in February and March, which are as follows: A black red hackle, with the above wings and body; a mallard wing, and the above body; a peacock harl body, a soot-coloured dun hackle, and a tip of gold. No. 10 hook.

There is a small fly, which I term the "heath fly," which is an excellent one in this month, and is made thus: The body is made of the fine fur of the belly of the hedgehog, or rat back fur (common rat), mixed with red squirrel fur, and a little orange mohair, rolled on thin and taper; a small silver grey hackle for legs, and winged with the grey tail feather of the partridge. A grey mallard and red squirrel fur makes another good fly. No. 10 hook.

No. 3. The Little Blue Dun.—The body is made of mole's fur, slightly mixed with bright yellow mohair, a light blue dun hackle for legs, and starling wings. No. 12 hook. This delicate little fly appears on cold days in March, and is well taken by the trout from ten till four in the evening, with the little red dun.

No. 4. The Orange Dun.—The body is made of orange and hare's fur, a honey dun hackle for legs, and grey mallard wings. No. 10 hook. Good on windy days in this month and the next. There should be but little hackle used on small flies in the early season, as the fur is sufficient or nearly so.

No. 5. The Marlow Buzz.—The body is made of peacock harl, a dun hackle over it from the tail, and two dark red ones round the shoulder, rib of silver. This fly does best where there are large trees growing over the river banks.

No. 6. The Brown Hackle.—The body is made of yellow brown mohair, a little orange fox fur, and two short fibred brown-red hackles rolled from the tail over the body, and ribbed with gold wire for evening fishing. It will be found a good one for large trout in river or lake, winged with hen pheasant tail, and forked with two fibres of the same feather, hook No. 10 for the small fly, and No. 6 for the larger size.

There is also a small red fly comes on in this month, very killing; the body is made of red squirrel's fur, a turn of a red hackle round the throat, and grey mallard wings mixed with partridge; hook No. 8.

FLIES FOR APRIL.

No. 7. The Soldier Fly.—The body is made of scarlet-colored mohair, ribbed with fine gold twist, and two black-red cock hackles run up over the body from the tail, (it is made also with orange floss silk body, ribbed with black silk), a small furnace hackle round the throat and a darkish starling wing. The dark red furnace hackle has a dark mark round the edges.

It may also be made to advantage with peacock harl and black-red hackles over it, and tipped with gold. The latter way makes it the "cochybonddu" of Wales. It kills best on windy days in general, with the cow-dung fly, and partridge hackle.

No. 8. The Cuckoo Hackle.—The body is made of peacock's harl, and two dark dun hackles, with darkish bars across them, rolled up to the throat; give it a tag of yellow green silk, at the end of the tail, silver.

The Granam fly may be made thus:—The wings are made of hen pheasant wing feather, hare's ear fur for body, and a grizzled cock hackle for legs. It is a four-winged fly, and when it flutters on the water it is very much like the engraving in the plate; but when it sails down the surface, the wings lie flat on its back, and as soon as it touches the water it drops its eggs; the trout take it freely for about a week in this month, with the gravel or spider fly,—dun body, black hackle, and woodcock wings; some use lead-coloured body.

No. 9. The Black Palmer, or Hackle.—The body is made of yellow floss silk, ribbed with silver tinsel, and two short fibred black hackles struck on from the tail to the shoulder. Hook No. 8.—Vary the body of this fly with peacock harl without the silver, and it will be a capital one for light clear water on No. 12 hook. Use the cow-dung fly on windy days, with the above-named one.

No. 10. The Dun Fox Fly.—The body is made of the fur found on the neck of the fox next the skin, mixed with golden yellow mohair. The wings are the wing feather of the starling or fieldfare, with two fibres of a stiff honey dun cock hackle for tail; pick out the fur a little at the shoulder for legs; hook No. 12. Never was there a better little fly than this thrown on the water, it will kill fish any day in the year. Put on the little black hackle, with peacock harl body with it as a drop fly; and when the dun fox is used as a drop fly, put on the March brown as a stretcher. There may be seen three shades of this fly on the water at the same time occasionally; the other two shades are the ash and blue fox,—the first is a very light dun colour of the fox cub's neck or face, the other is of a darker blue shade; they are great favorites with the trout, artificially; in mild weather throughout the summer, a small wren and grouse hackle may be used with them, the bodies made very thin and taper, and rather full at the shoulder—the wren with orange mohair body, and the grouse with golden yellow floss silk body.

No. 11. The Dun Drake.—The body is made of golden olive mohair, mixed with hare's ear fur, the light and dark, and forked with two short fibres of brown mallard. The wings are made of land-rail wing, and a little brown mallard, mixed nicely together. Hook, No. 9. There is a dark red, and a dark dun fly on the water at the same time as the dun-drake, all of which will be found good ones till the end of May. The Irish name for the dun drake, is "Coughlan,"[1] made thus:—The wings, grey partridge tail; the body, light brown bear's fur, with bright yellow mohair, hare's fur from the face, mixed altogether, forked with two stripes of a dark mallard's feather, and a partridge hackle. No. 8 hook. In Ireland they consider this the most useful fly they have in April and May, as a stretcher, used with the little dun fox, and black-red, (soldier fly).

No. 12. The Stone Fly.—The body is made of brown mohair ribbed with yellow silk, a tuft or tag of yellow mohair or silk at the tail, and a little yellow mohair worked in under the shoulder, over which roll the hackle, which should be of a brown-red colour; the wings are made of the hen pheasant tail mixed with copper brown mallard, made full, and larger than the body. No. 6 hook. If this fly is made of good colours, as above described, hardly any large trout, in humour of taking, can well refuse it. An odd one of them may be seen in March, when the weather is mild; but in April and May, when it becomes more congenial to them, they appear numerous towards the evening. Ribbed with gold twist, it makes a famous grilse fly.

No. 13. The Yellow Sally.—The body is made of buff-colored fur, and a small yellow hackle for legs round the head; the wings are made of the buff-coloured feather inside the wing of the thrush. No. 13 hook. This is the forerunner of the Green Drake or May fly. The trout take this little fly freely, and it is a most excellent killer on fine days, if made according to the description. It will be found on the water till the end of May. The partridge hackle is also good in this month.

---

[1] **FOOTNOTE:** "Taylor's Angler."

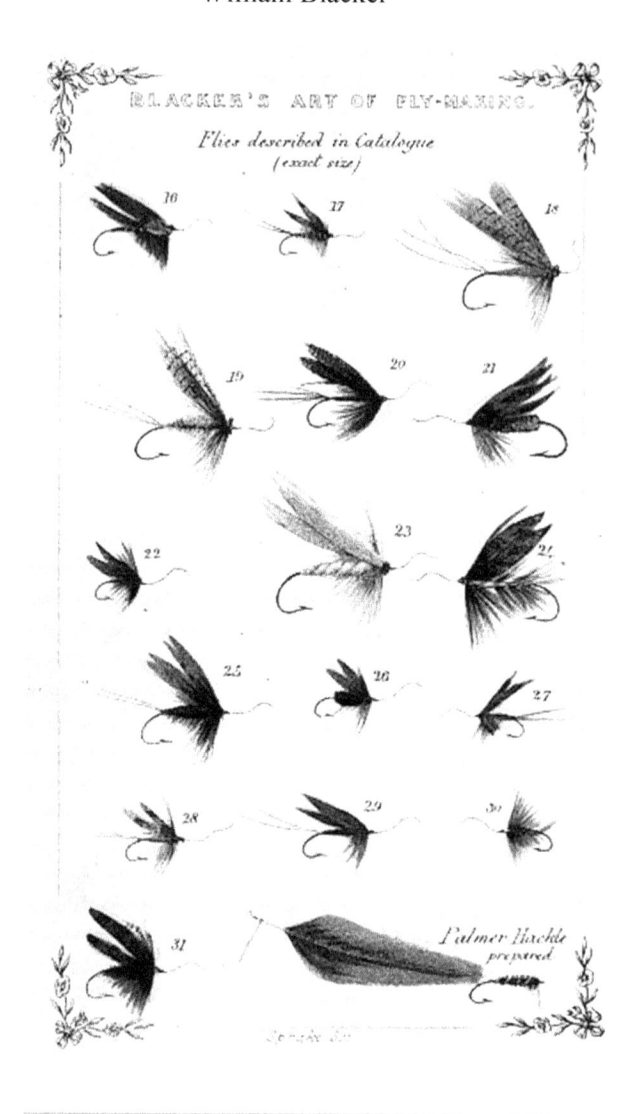

FLIES FOR MAY.

No. 14. The Black Gnat.—The body is made of black hair from the spaniel's ear which is fine and soft, or a black ostrich feather clipped very close, and a small black hackle for legs; the wings are from the starling's wing feather. No. 13 hook. This is a good fly throughout a clear day, used as a dropper with the foregoing fly, and wren tail.

It floats on the surface of the water in numbers on sultry days with mild showers of rain. It may be varied to advantage with blue silk body.

No. 15. The Little Brown Midge.—The body is made of brown mohair with a shade of orange mohair at the shoulder, two turns of a small brown-red hackle for legs; the wings are made of brown mallard and a little strip of land-rail mixed. No. 13 hook, snick bend.

There appears to be a variety of small flies on the water with the above fly about the middle of the day, dark browns, pea-greens, and dun flies, all water insects, which the trout take very freely.

No. 16. The Little Iron Blue.—The body is made of a little light coloured water-rat's fur mixed with a few hairs of yellow, an iron blue coloured dun hackle for legs, and the wings from a blue dun feather to be found underneath the wing of a dun hen, or starling wing feather, tail it with a dun hackle, two fibres. No. 10 hook. It sails upright on its legs on the water, with both tail and wings cocked up, so that it would suit best as a bob fly. It will be found a useful fly throughout the season, varied a little in shade according to the weather, the darker ones on fine clear days.

The Coachman, Oral, and the Governor flies will be found good ones in this month towards night, when the beautiful White Moth may be also seen.

No. 17. Hare's Ear and Yellow.—The body is made of the light part of the fur from the hare's ear, ribbed with yellow silk; the wings are from the wing of the starling or fieldfare, and two stiff fibres of honey dun cock's hackle, from the rump for tail, to cock up, pick out the fur at the head for legs, No. 12 hook. It will kill fish every day in this month, and will be found good till the end of July. It may be also called the Little Cocktail.

No. 18. The Green Drake.—The body of this beautiful fly is made of yellow green mohair, the color of a gosling newly come out of the shell, and ribbed with yellow-brown silk, a shade of light brown mohair at the tail, and a tuft of the same color at the shoulder, picked out between the hackle, the whisks of the tail to be of three black hairs of the mane of a horse, about three-quarters of an inch long; the hackle to be a greenish buff dyed, (dye a silver dun hackle with bars across it called a cuckoo), or a light ginger hackle bordering on a yellow. The wings, which should be made full, and to stand upright, are made of dyed mallard feathers of a greenish buff, or yellowish shade: a brown head of peacock harl tied neatly above the wings, No. 6 hook. The wings may be made of the ends of two large dyed mallard feathers, with each side stripped off, and the beautiful long ends to form the wings, tie them on whole back to back, a little longer than the bend of the hook—these feathers stand up well and appear very natural in the water; large size ones kill well in lakes, with bright yellow mohair bodies and gold twist rolled up them; a long honey dun palmer kills well on windy days, allowed to sink near the bottom, ribbed with gold twist (see the palmer in the plate with double hook). The trout take it no doubt for the Creeper or "Cad Bait;" a very small swivel tied on at the head, would improve its life-like appearance in the water as you move it with the rod; and the larger size one would also do better with a swivel.

No. 19.—The Grey Drake.—The body is made of pale yellow mohair, or floss, three fibres of dark mallard for tail, ribbed with brown silk, a grizzled dun-cock's hackle for legs, or silver grey; grey mallard for wings, and a peacock harl head.

The body should be made taper, and full at the head, it is a capital fly on rough days in May and June, and used to advantage on warm evenings. The body may be also made of dun fox fur, grey at the ends, a silver grey hackle for legs, and forked with three hairs from a fitch's tail; the wings grey mallard and widgeon mixed. It is also made of straw body, grey cock's hackle, and mallard wings—these two methods are very good. They kill well in Scotland, and in Ireland are called the "Grey Cochlan." These flies may be seen in "Taylor's Angler."

Mr. Taylor was an angler of no small pretensions, he was very fond of the Irish coloured flies, and has adopted many of them as standards for Scotland, England, and many rivers in Wales.

FLIES FOR JUNE.

No. 20.—The Great Red Spinner.—The body is made of red mohair, ribbed with fine gold wire, and a red cock hackle for legs; the wings are made of brown and grey mallard, the grey underneath; two fibres of stiff cock's saddle hackle for tail, No. 6 or 7 hook. The Small Red Spinner is made as the above, but instead of mallard use starling wings. It is an excellent fly for a dark evening in June and July, with the furnace hackle.

No. 21.—The Alder Fly.—The body is made of brown coloured peacock harl, a black-red cock hackle for legs, the wings are made of hen pheasant tail feathers, hook No 6. There is another way or two of making this fly which cannot be beaten, they are mostly used in Ireland, and are known to be killers in England and Scotland. The body is made of bronze brown mohair, a very small brown grouse hackle round the head, and the wings from a brown spotted hen's wing, No. 8 hook. The other is made with grey and red partridge tail mixed for wings, a copper brown peacock harl body, and a dark brown red hackle off a cock's neck for legs. The legs may be also made of the wren's tail or woodcock hackle, this feather is found on the roots of the outside of the wings of the woodcock. These are good flies in lakes or rivers for large trout—rib with gold for lakes.

No. 22.—The Sand Fly.—The body is made of the sandy coloured fur from the hare's pole, mixed with orange mohair, and a small ginger coloured cock's hackle for legs; the wings are made of a sandy coloured brown hen's wing, No. 10 hook. An excellent little fly on fine days with a little wind and occasional showers.

There is another little fly that will be found equally good, made thus:—the wings are made of red and grey partridge tail feathers, orange body, and black-red hackle rolled up from the tail to the head, it will kill well on dark days, ribbed with gold, No. 8 hook.

No. 23.—The White Moth.—The body is made of white mohair, which is lively ribbed with orange floss, a white cock's hackle rolled round the shoulder; the wings from a white feather of the swan that grows over the back. It may be varied with cream coloured mohair, very light ginger hackle, and a buff wing from a hen of that colour; and a browner one may be made from a matted brown hen's wing, or light brown grouse tail, or large hackle off the rump of the same bird, brown-red cock's hackle, the whole to be made full, of good coloured and stiff materials, that they may not absorb the water, and alight heavy when thrown on the surface.

No. 24. The Oak Fly.—The body is made of orange silk, and a little hare's ear fur under the shoulder, rib it with a furnace hackle from the centre of the body up (if the hackles are tied on at the tail they are very apt to get cut with the teeth of the fish in a very short time). The wings may be made from the mottled brown hen, or the woodcock wings, of a red tinge. No. 8 hook. This fly cannot be too highly valued for its killing qualities. It will be found useful for large trout of a windy day with a grey cloud over head, and not likely to rain. "Mr. Bowlker," in his "Art of Angling," mentions the oak fly in this manner: "The oak, ash, woodcock, cannon, or down-hill fly, comes on about the sixteenth of May, and continues on till about a week in June; it is to be found on the butts of trees, with its head always downwards, which gives it the name of the down-hill fly. It is bred in oak-apples, and is the best of all flies for bobbing at the bush in the natural way, and a good fly for the dab-line, when made artificially." The wings are made from a feather out of the wing of the partridge or woodcock, the body with a bittern's feather, and the head with a little of the brown part of hare's fur. The hook, No. 6. Some dub it with an orange, tawny, and black ground, and with blackish wool and gold twist; the wings off the brown part of a mallard's feather.

FLIES FOR JULY.

No. 25.—The Great Whirling Dun.—The body is made of water-rat's fur, mixed with yellow mohair, and ribbed with yellow silk; a reddish blue dun hackle for legs; grey mallard wings, or starling—try both. No. 8 hook. There are two or three varieties of this fly, which make their appearance in this month, and are very killing on fine, mild days, with occasional showers; their colours run from a dark to a light sky-blue.

"Mr. Bowlker," in his "Art of Angling," an authority which I like, as he was himself a fisherman, speaks thus of one of these beautiful flies: "It comes on about the end of May, and continues till the middle of July. It is a neat, curious, and beautiful fly; its wings are transparent, stand upright on its back, and are of a fine blue colour, its body is of a pale yellow, its tail forked, and the colour of its wings. It is a fly that the fishes take extremely well from seven o'clock in the evening till sun-set. The wings are made from the light blue feather of a hen; the body is made with pale yellow mohair, mixed with light blue fur, and ribbed with a fine cock's hackle, dyed yellow, the hook, No. 8." This is taken from "Bowlker's" original work.

No. 26. The Little Peacock Fly.—The body is made of bright brown peacock's harl, with a tip of gold at the tail, or gold colour floss silk; a red hackle for legs, and a starling wing. This little fly comes on about the middle of July, and continues till the end of August. It may be used to advantage on fine days, with the blue dun, and cinnamon brown. I have seen this latter fly on the river "Mole," in August, of a fine brown colour, and plump in the body, about the size of the Great Whirling Dun. The body was red brown, the legs an amber brown, the wings were a mottled light brown, and the tail of the same colour as the wings. I have seen the above fly some time after on the "Bann," in the north of Ireland, a river six times the size of the Mole, not half the size, in August. This circumstance of the difference in size, must be the nature of the soil through which the rivers flow; the "Bann" is a gravelly bed, full of large stones, with a very fall strong running stream; the "Mole" not so. It is my opinion that in the summer months there is more sport to be had with flies as small as can be made, than with the general run, except late in the evening, then use a large fly—a brown, or white moth, where a large fish shows himself.

No. 27. The Blue Blow.—The body is made of mole's fur mixed with yellow mohair, run very taper from the tail up; the wings are made of a tom-tit's tail feather, or water hen; the tail is two hairs of a mouse's whisker, or fibres of dark dun hackle; the body is picked out a little at the head to imitate legs; the fly altogether to be made very small and delicate, hook No. 13. These little flies may be seen on good size rivers in hundreds, in the summer on sultry days; where there is a stone projecting out of the water they gather round it, and with the motion are carried up and down on the side of the stone, where large trout lie, like ant bears, sucking them in by the dozen; the wing of the water-rail is capital to imitate that of the fly. There is another excellent killing fly that may be used with the above, made thus;—body, gold colour mohair; tip of gold; woodcock or wren hackle for legs; grey partridge tail for wrings; and two fibres of the same for tail; No. 10 hook. They are good where the river is low, and are excellent till the end of August, used with the little brown fly, and ash fox.

There are also three little flies which are very good in this month and the next, and although they are not very well known by name, nevertheless they will be found killing. First, the "Orange Wren," with orange mohair body, and wren tail hackle. Second, the "Golden Wren," with golden yellow mohair body, and wren tail hackle for legs. Third, the "Green Wren," with green floss body, and wren tail for legs. The Brown Wren, and the little Peacock Wren, are also good. No. 13 hook. The latter little fly is called the "Shiner."

No. 28. The Yellow Dun.—The body is made of light buff-coloured fur, white sable far dyed yellow, and a honey dun cock's hackle for legs; two fibres of the same feather for tail; the wings are made of starling wing feather. No. 12 hook. This pretty little fly is a great favourite with the trout in the evenings of sultry days, till the end of August and September.

FLIES FOR AUGUST.

No. 29. The Red Dun.—The body is made of red orange hair, over which roll a small dun hackle; the wings are a dun grey, and are made of starling wing feather, mixed with a little mallard. No. 10 hook. It may be varied thus: Red legs and dun body; orange floss body, over which roll a black hackle, and starling wing. The size of hook to vary from No. 10 to No. 7.

This is an excellent fly in rapid streams where there are large trout; it is so attractive that they cannot refuse it when it moves over them. Trout that lie or haunt strong streams, are called, in Ireland, "Hunters." The cause is, no doubt, through their being thin and long in the body, and are possessed with enormous mouths to take in their prey. They take small trout freely.

No. 30. The Ant Fly.—The body is made of brown floss silk, and a small fibred peacock harl at tail; a brown red hackle for legs, and wings of starling feather. No. 10 hook.

There is a black ant the same size as the above, and a red and black one much larger; the black one is made of black floss for the body, small black hackle for legs, and a blackbird's wing for the wings of the fly. The small ones kill on fine days, and the larger ones when there is a strong wind, which blows them on the water, and causes a ripple.

Blacker's Art of Fly Making, &c.,

No. 31. The Caperer.—The body is made of brown mohair, or floss silk of a copper colour, and tipped with gold at the tail; a brown red cock's hackle at the shoulder for legs, and winged with the woodcock wing feather. No. 8 hook. This fly may be seen on fine sultry days whirling up and down over the water, and occasionally dipping on the surface; the trout take them very freely. This fly will be found on the water till the end of September, with the paler dun, yellow dun, blue dun, and willow fly. The greyling also like these little flies.

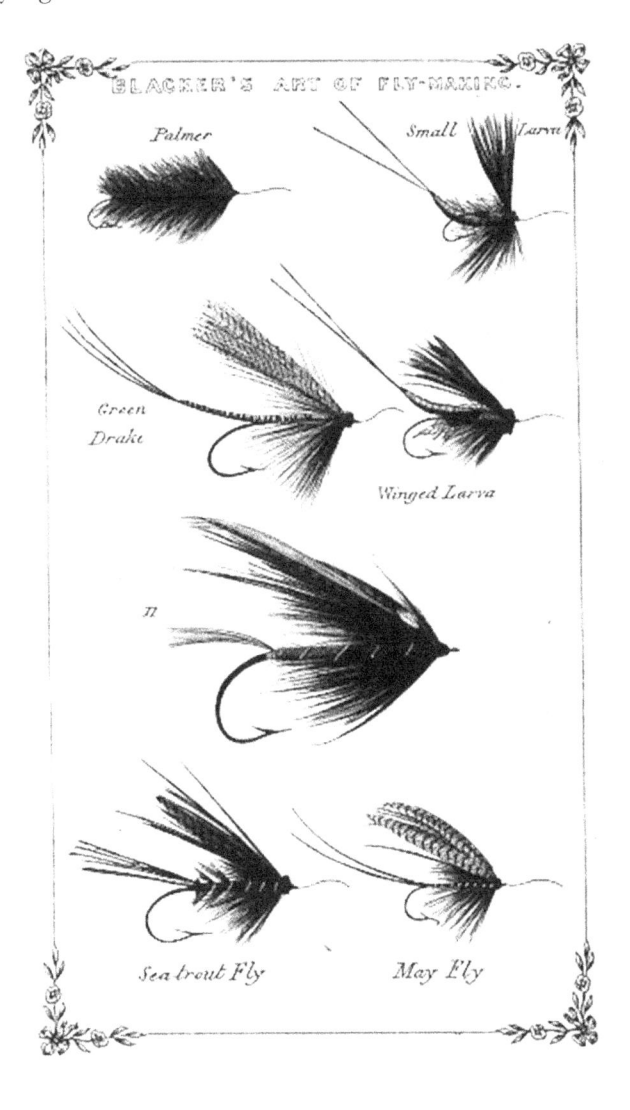

The Winged Larva.—The body is made of brown mohair; the larva is attached to this body at the shoulder, and tailed with two fibres of golden pheasant neck feather, a woodcock hackle round the shoulder, and winged with hen pheasant tail, mixed with a little woodcock or partridge tail feather, and a bronze peacock head. No. 8 hook. It will be found a good fly on dark windy days in this month and the next, and during the prevalence of winds from the east; it will do best where a strong rapid stream runs into a deep pool.

A Substitute for the Winged Larva:—The body is made of bright golden yellow mohair, which looks very transparent; a woodcock wing, and a hackle off the same bird, with two fibres of golden pheasant neck feather for tail. No. 8 hook.

The Willow Flies.—The body of the first is made of blue squirrel's fur, mixed with a little yellow mohair; a blue dun cock's hackle round the shoulder, and a tomtit wing. No. 8 hook. The second fly is made of orange silk body, ribbed with fine black silk; a very dark furnace hackle round the head, and blackbird's wing. No. 10 hook. The third fly is made of the wings or blue feather of the sea-swallow, for the wing of the fly, and the lightest blue fur that can be got for body (the fine blue of the fox's neck, next to the skin; the fur of a very young water-rat, or the lightest blue fur of the squirrel); a light dun cock's hackle, and a tail of the same. No. 10 hook. These little flies will kill till the end of October, and are excellent fur greyling. There are hundreds of other flies that make their appearance on the water through the summer months, which come under the angler's notice when in pursuit of his pastime, that may be imitated to advantage, the varieties of which must fill the mind with admiration.

FISHING RODS AND FLY FISHING.

For a trout rod, to have a good balance from the butt to the extreme top, it is essentially necessary that the wood should be well-seasoned, straight in the grain, and free from knots and imperfections. It should consist of three or four joints, according to fancy. There is not the least occasion for a rod to be glued up in pieces first, and then cut into lengths and fitted with ferrules, for then you have the unnecessary trouble of lapping the splices, but it is best to clean each piece separately, and measure the exact taper each piece should be to one another with the ferrules to fit in the same proportion, the least thing wider at the lower end than at the top; the ends to be bored for the tongues to fit into tightly to prevent shaking, that when they are double brazed they may fit airtight.

The ends must be bored previous to planing down the substance of the pieces, and tied round with waxed thread to prevent them from opening or cracking, so that these pieces may be pushed into each end of the boring whilst the rod is planed up to its proper substance or size, except the tops, which should be well glued-up pieces of bamboo cane, and filed down to their proper sizes to suit the other parts of the rod; this may be also done by fastening the tongue of the top in the bored joint next in size. The butt should be made of ash, the middle piece of hickory, and the top of bamboo, which is the lightest and toughest of all woods that can be brought to so fine a consistency. The length of the rod for single-hand fly fishing should be from twelve to thirteen feet long—a length which may be used with great facility without tiring the arm. The butt should be easy in the grasp and not a great deal of timber in it; the next piece to be nearly as stout as the butt above the ferrule for a foot and a half, this prevents its being weak at that particular part, which otherwise would cause the rod to be limber in the middle; the next or fourth piece to be stiffer and lighter in the wood to keep up the top; the whole rod to stand nearly straight up when held in the hand, and to have a smart spring above, which assists materially in getting out the line when throwing. The splices of the tops should be tightly bound over with the finest silk, well waxed, and over all three or four coats of good varnish that is not liable to crack. You cannot bind the splices tight enough with coarse three-cord silk, the top being so small it cannot be drawn together near so well as with fine silk, and when the varnish rubs off it opens and admits the water, which loosens the glued splice inside. The fine waxed silk is to be preferred by all means, as it lies closer on the wood, becomes harder, and makes the splice stiffer to work with the other parts.

When the whole is ringed, ferruled, and fitted for the reel complete, it should not (a twelve foot) exceed one pound; it will afford great comfort to the fly fisher in his innocent pursuit, and will not fatigue him during a long summer day. The reel should be light, in proportion to the rod, and to contain thirty yards of silk and hair line made fine and taper, and when the rod is grasped in the hand a little way above the reel, the balance should be the same above the hand as below it, so that it may be used with the greatest ease.

The beautiful rent and glued-up bamboo-cane fly rods, which I turn out to the greatest perfection, are very valuable, as they are both light and powerful, and throw the line with great facility. The cane for these rods must be of the very best description, or they will not last any time. They will last for years if properly made, and of course the fisher must take care of them; they are best when made into pocket rods, in eight joints, with all the knots cut out, and the good pieces between each knot rent and glued up; these may be had in my shop of as good a balance as a three-joint rod, most superbly made of the lightest brazings. They make capital perch and roach rods with a bait top added to the extra fly top, with bored butt to hold all. These rods can be made to suit a lady's hand for either boat or fly fishing.

The salmon rod should be made in four pieces or joints. The butt of the best long grained solid ash, the wood of which is not so heavy as hickory, and is not liable to break at the ferrule, that is, if the ferrule is put on "flush," without letting it into the wood by scoring it; the piece above the butt, and the joint next the top, should be of the very best well-seasoned hickory, without crack or flaw; the tops to be made of the best yellow bamboo cane, either rent and glued up in three pieces, or spliced in short lengths with the knots cut away; the first joint to be nearly as stout as the substance of the wood above the ferrule as the end of the butt for a foot and a half, to prevent the rod being limber in the middle; the next joint that holds the top should be very smart, and come up at a touch when bent with the hand, and the extreme lightness of the cane top prevents all appearance of its being top-heavy, which cannot be prevented with lance-wood, unless it is made very fine indeed, and then it becomes useless. The length of the rod should not exceed seventeen or eighteen feet long, and for light rivers, sixteen feet is quite long enough; if the angler fly fishes for salmon from a boat, fourteen feet will be sufficient, made, of course, very powerful throughout, as in some large rivers a salmon will take the fly close to the boat in strong and deep streams. The rings should be pretty large, to admit of the line running freely, and the joints double brazed, which prevents the bare wood of the tongues twisting off when the rod is taken to pieces after a day's fishing, particularly when they get wet. The reel fittings should be about a foot and a half, or say twenty inches from the extreme end, that there may be room for the left hand to grasp it easily below the reel, which prevents the rod hanging heavy on the arms, and will balance it much better than having the reel too near the end of the butt. When the salmon rod is bent after playing a fish, it can be easily straightened by turning it when the next fish is hooked, and allow the line to run through the rings on the top of the rod; by holding it in that position, you can see how you are winding up the line on the reel, and regulate it according as the fish runs towards you, for if the reel is held underneath when the fish is on, if he runs towards you, it cannot be seen whether the line runs on in a lump or not, which, if it does, often causes it to stop, and may occasion the loss of your fish.

The most essential and nicest point of all is in casting the line and trout flies neatly on the water, which, when properly accomplished in a masterly way, will be the greatest means towards the success of the fly fisher in hooking and catching his fish. In the first place, the fisher should keep as far off the water as possible when throwing next his own side, and make it a rule, whenever he can, to angle on the bank from which the wind blows, as it will enable him to throw the flies across to the opposite bank, and play them gently down the stream in a slanting direction towards him, moving backwards as they approach his side, drawing them up along the bank if the stream is any ways deep, as a trout of good size is often lying in such a place when undisturbed, as you fish cautiously down.

The line should not be let off the reel too fast when you begin to throw, that the stream may be carefully covered near you, and as you move along let it off so as to cover the whole of the water. Hold the rod firmly above the reel in the right hand, and take hold of the end of the casting line in the left, give it a motion towards your left shoulder, and over the head with a circle to the full length of the flies behind you, and with a spring of the rod and motion of the arm bring them right before you on to the stream, as straightly and lightly as possible, and by this method you will prevent them whipping off behind in a very short time; allow the line always to stretch to its full length behind, and keep them on the move, with the backward sweep of the rod round the head propel them forward to the place you desire they should fall, and I do not doubt that you will make neither splash nor ripple on the surface. And when a fish makes a rise, move the rod upwards with a gentle pull, which is better than striking hard, as the small hook is easily driven, and there is no occasion to break the hold or line. Never hold too hard on a large fish, but let him run if he will, a small one may be landed immediately. By no means attempt to go "an angling" without a landing net, as there may be danger in losing your fish, after having the trouble or sport of playing him a long time, and the bank high on your side. I have been always in the habit of fishing down the stream, throwing my flies slantingly to the opposite bank, and letting them fall gradually with the current, and walking slowly along lifting and throwing them at my leisure—it is all fancy whether up or down you go, so as it is well done—what you have habituated yourself to in fly fishing in general, that do. Keep your shadow as much as possible off the water, and when you land your fish let his head drop into the net first, and his whole weight will follow, lift him clean up on the bank with a pull of the net towards you, as this prevents him dropping out.

FLY-FISHING FOR SALMON.

When you begin fly-fishing for Salmon, you must be careful not to let out too much of the reel line first, but when you become accustomed to it, and are master of throwing a short one, let it out gradually till you are enabled to cover the pool over which you cast with ease.

If you practice throwing over a smooth wide part of the river, you will see how your line falls on the water, whether thrown in a lump, or light and straight without a splash; but at one time you may cast the line right out over the stream at its full length, and on giving another cast you may allow the line to fall on the water in the middle of it first, and the fly to fall last, which is not so good, but in either way the fish will rise and take it; by the last cast you may get the line farther off, and the fly alighting near the opposite bank, it is very apt to be taken by a fish lying close under it; and when throwing, keep the point of the rod up out of the water, and do not let it strike it; throw across in a rather slanting direction, allowing the fly to sweep down without a curve in the middle of the line, and at the same time move the rod playfully to give the fly a life-like appearance; drawing it in towards your side of the bank, moving it up and down gradually with the current, and when a fish takes the fly raise your hand, and fasten the hook without a jerk, holding up your rod at the same time with what is termed a "sweet fast," that it may not get slack at any time till you have killed him; when you poise the rod in your hands for a throw, the whole knack is in keeping the left hand steady, and with a turn of the right hand cause the line to make a circle round the left shoulder and over the head, propel it forward with the spring of the rod, keeping the fly going all the time till it falls on the water before you as straight as possible; when you lift the fly out of the water to throw again, you require to make use of the strength of the right arm, giving it the proper turn round with the wrist, making a sweep of the extent of the line behind you, and with the spring and power of the rod direct the fly on that part of the stream where you desire it should fall; letting the line out occasionally off the reel with your hand, which gives the fly a very natural motion on the water, moving it gradually down towards your side, when you lift the line out and make another throw as before a little lower down, and so on until you cover the whole stream.

You may change to the left hand when you are tired with the right, or according to the side you are fishing from, to facilitate and ease your exertion as much as possible when throwing a long line. When I have happened to be in a barn at a farm house on the river side, I have often thought when taking up the flail to thrash awhile, whilst the man was resting himself, that the exertion was remarkably like throwing the fly with the Salmon rod, the whole method appears to be in the turn of the wrist and arm, for when the flail is raised up and wound over the left shoulder, with a certain impulse known to one's self you propel it forward over the head, striking the sheaf on the ground with full force on any part you like, where you think there are any ears in it.

Many may not be acquainted with flail thrashing, but were they to understand the knack, it is easily done; so, also, is the using of the salmon rod, with a little practice, and observing a good thrower if you happen to meet one on the river, or an old fisherman you employ.

Keep yourself steady on your feet, and your body well up when casting, as it gives more power to the muscles, and when a salmon is fairly hooked it will prevent your being nervous or striking too quick, but as I said before, rise your hand and keep the line taut; as the fish will often rise several times out of the water in succession when first pricked with the hook, on finding himself detained; when he runs keep the rod nearly perpendicular, as the spring of it will soon tire him out; if he is a good way off and makes a rush towards you, wind up your line quickly, keeping it taut at the same time, and moving backwards till he is near your own shore: if he rolls over in the water apply the gaff and lift him out, but if he is not regularly beat he will rush off again on seeing the gaff with great strength, give in he must at last by the gentle strain of the rod that is always upon him. He often gets sulky, and lies down on the bottom of the river, when it will be found difficult to start him again: a clearing ring let down the line on his nose will cause him to run, and when he does so, it is best to bear stronger upon him, as in so doing you have the best chance of quickly tiring and capturing him. I think it the best plan to lay the gaff under him, and gaff him in the gills, which prevents tearing or making a hole in the fish.

The Salmon reel should be made of the lightest and hardest material, not too much contracted, but a good width, that the line may be wound up evenly without incumbrance; a plain upright handle is much the safest when playing a fish, as the portable ones are apt to crack or snap off if they meet the least obstruction in the running out of the line; and the portable handle stands too far out, which catches the line almost every time it is drawn off or a cast given. Small reels may be made with portable handles, without any fear of their breaking, as the fish are small and can be managed easily.

The salmon line should be of silk and hair eight-plait or four-plait, eighty or a hundred yards long, and for small rivers, sixty yards for a sixteen feet rod. The casting line for clear waters should be half treble and half single gut, to suit grilse or small salmon flies in summer; and in the spring of the year when large flies are in use, good strong-twisted gut, three yards long, is what is necessary for a heavy reel line, particularly in large rivers, as the Shannon and the Bann in Ireland, and the Tweed in Scotland.

There are not three better Salmon Rivers in the world than the above, were the salmon allowed access into them during the summer months for the amusement of those great angling gentlemen who would visit them during that period, or even if there were but a few let up past the "cruives" or "cuts," that there might be a sprinkling for them to throw flies over. It would not matter to them what nets the fishermen along the shores of the estuaries used, as they only affect the "Cruives," or "Fixed Traps" built across the rivers, as of course less fish run into them, and there would be abundance of salmon and grilse go up the centre or deep part of the river, which the fishermen could not possibly reach.

These "Traps" are kept down all the summer, from the early spring till the end of August, at which period they are what is termed "lifted," and up run the spawning fish; and the great fly fishers now lay by their rods and tackle for that season, as fly fishing is prohibited when the salmon are spawning in the rivers. There is certainly a respite in the Tweed, when the nets are taken off at the end of the season for the accommodation of the fly fisher; and were it so in the Shannon and the Bann, there would be very great satisfaction in having a month or six weeks' fishing in these splendid rivers. They are certainly free throughout the summer to the fly fisher, but he might labour a whole day with his rod and fly without getting a rise, except by chance.

There will never be any good done until the "cruives" or "cuts" are removed off the rivers, unless the head landlord would make an agreement with the renter of the "cruive," and enforce it as a law,—to lift the "cruive" two days in the week, that there might be fish in the rivers for the accommodation of the great body of gentlemen anglers who make it their business to travel to these rivers to find amusement in Fly Fishing, at very great expense; although I do not know if even this would do,—it would be best by all means to remove them; and, independent of fair netting for the general supply at the mouths and estuaries, a Society of Anglers could rent the entire river, were the owner to meet them on liberal terms which no doubt he would, and this would prevent the destruction by degrees of the best breeding-fish in the river.

AN ACCOUNT OF THE SALMON, AND ITS VARIETIES.

I desire merely to give some account of this beautiful fish for the information of my readers, the knowledge of which has come under my own notice, in the rivers of Ireland in particular, amongst the fishermen at their mouths, at the "cruives" or "cuts," and throughout my rambles along their banks.

This excellent salmon is a very handsome fish, the head is small, the body rather long and covered with bright scales, the back is of a bluish shade, the other parts white, and marked with irregular dark brown spots on the head, the covers of the gills, down each side from the lateral lines to near the edge of the back, very few are to be seen below the lines which run from head to tail; the tail is forked.

He takes great delight in pursuing small fish and fry, and in playing and jumping on the top of the water, at insects no doubt, and for his own sport.

It has been often said that there was never any thing found in the salmon's stomach such as edibles, but it has been recently discovered that they prey upon herrings, sprats, fry, and other dainties in their native element; and as these fish are very nutritious and fat in themselves, no doubt the nourishing channel in them receives the substance of the food very quickly, as it appears to be digested so rapidly in their stomachs. He leaves the sea for the fresh water rivers about January and February, and continues to run up till September and October, their spawning time, and some spawn after this time; they are often big with roe in December and January, in the end of August or the beginning of September; when they are in roe regularly, they cannot be in proper season; they get soft, their beautiful color and spots vanish, and they do not appear like the same fish. They travel up rivers as far as they can possibly get, into lakes and their feeders, and tributaries of large rivers, where they take delight in the broad gravelly fords, and strong deep running currents, which they like to be as clear as crystal, to effect which they will leap over weirs, waterfalls, "cuts," "cruives," and "traps," when there is a flood rushing over them, to the great delight of the fly fisher, who loves to see them run and escape these obstructions.

The male fish is supplied by nature with a hard gristly beak on the end of the under jaw, which fits into a socket in the upper jaw to a nicety; with this the Salmon go to work with their heads up stream, rising their tails sometimes nearly perpendicular, and root up the sand and gravel in heaps, leaving a hollow between, wherein the female deposits the eggs; the male fish still performing his part, chasing away the large trout that are ready to root it up (the spawn), he covers it over substantially against the forthcoming winter's floods and storms. By this time he becomes wearied, spent, and sickly, and then turns himself round and makes head for the sea, where, if once happily arrived, he soon makes up for the debility in his blue, his fresh, and ever free element. The refreshing and purging nature of the salt water soon makes him once more strong and healthy, he may be seen leaping and playing in the sea near the river's mouth on his recovery. I have been told by fishermen that they proceed in shoals to the ice fields in the North Seas, and return to the rivers and estuaries in the spring and summer as they departed, in large shoals; they discover themselves in the bays by jumping out of the water as they near the river.

The Salmon haunts the deepest, strongest, and most rapid rivers, and is rarely to be seen in those wherein there is much traffic, or that are sullen or muddy. They prefer the upper parts of rough streams that run into large pools, and the tails of these pools, behind large stones, in the middle and at sides of waterfalls in the eddies, these are the parts to throw for them, but the fisherman on the water will show the angler all the best places. The best months to angle for them are from March till the middle of August, after September they are out of season. They will take the fly best from six or seven o'clock in the morning till nine, and from three in the afternoon till dark, with a good wind blowing up stream. I have hooked them on the very top of a precipice, after surmounting the leap, where they lie to rest in the first deep pool they come to; they generally run down over the rocks or falls of water to the pool beneath, when they often get killed by the rapid descent.

THE SALMON FRY.

These beautiful little fish, the production of the spawn of the salmon, make their appearance in March and April, and if a flood happens to rise or swell the rivers about the end of the latter month, they are taken down in great numbers, till at last they enter the brackish water, where they grow in a short time as large as white trout. The salt water adds much to their growth. In the following spring and summer they run up the rivers in great quantities if they are allowed, and return to the sea again before winter. On their second return up the rivers they will be grown very large, and are then called "Grilse," or "Peals," &c.

There is a Salmon Trout of the same species, which is rounder in proportion to the Salmon, of a reddish hue when in season; it has small fine scales, beautifully intermixed with rich red and black spots on both sides of the lateral lines, from head to tail, and its handsome head is spotted over, as also the covers of the gills; the tail is shorter, and not so much forked as the salmon, and the fins are very strong. The flesh is most delicious, and some prefer it to salmon. They may be seen in the Fishmongers' shops from May till the end of August.

Another species is the Sewen of Wales, the White Trout of Ireland and England, and the Whiting of Scotland; they are very bright in colour, and run about the size of Mackerel; they haunt the roughest, strong streams, and gravelly bottoms. When they are hooked on the fly they will spring repeatedly out of the water, and afford pleasant sport for the angler. They take small gaudy flies like the Salmon Trout, and when the water is low, dun flies, black hackle flies with silver ribs, and grouse hackles of a light brown colour and yellow bodies. The hooks about Nos. 6 and 8.

Another species is the Bull-Trout, which has a short thick head, and a brownish body, covered with spots of a brown colour, and are found in all rivers having communication with the sea, and their tributaries, if there are no obstructions to prevent their running up. They are found running up the rivers in June and July, and in these months and August, are in good season. They are rather a dry fish.

The Par or Last-Spring are most plentiful in salmon rivers from May till the end of August, and are very much like the salmon fry, only for the dark bars across them, and towards the end of the season they are variously marked. There is no little fish so plump and lively when taken with the fly, except the Salmon Fry. As the Sea-Trout are known to grow to the weight of sixteen and twenty pounds in large rivers, such as the Tweed, the Shannon, and the Bann, the Par may be the fry of these fish, which run up the rivers in the spring and summer. These Sea-Trout differ much in shape and colour to the real Salmon, and are what are termed Salmon in the London markets.—This I heard from a fisherman at the mouth of the Tweed, who pointed out a large creel full to me, just taken in the nets, and amongst the whole there was but one Salmon. The Sea-Trout may be known by being paler, and covered with more spots, and by being longer and thinner in the body; the head is also much longer.

There is a rich golden hue over the Salmon when you get a side look of it; the body is plump and boar-backed, the head is very small, and there are few spots, except above the lateral lines.

I have seen the Par so numerous in the River Dovey, in Wales, that a man (a guide), took my salmon rod, and a cast of four small flies, the sun shining, and in two hours he killed nine pounds weight of these fish, about a finger in length or less. It perfectly surprised me; but it seems that this was but a small quantity in comparison to what the fishers were in the habit of taking out in a day. It appeared so, as the inn-keeper's wife potted them in large jars. These rivers abound with Sewen, Sea-Trout, and White Trout; the first-named fish is the White Trout of Wales, which corresponds with the Irish fish of that name, and called in Wales, Sewen. The Par may be the fry of these fish, which are of the Salmon species, and ought to be protected by law.

William Blacker

A DESCRIPTION OF THE FIFTEEN SALMON FLIES ENGRAVED IN THE PLATES.

These fifteen Salmon Flies may be considered by my readers as specimens of real perfection, and the "dons" of the present time amongst the great Salmon fishers. There is such a combination of colours in them throughout, that they will be found most killing in the rivers of Scotland and Ireland, if made on hooks of sizes to suit each, and their proper seasons.

I have taken the greatest pains imaginable to make them in proportion, and of the most choice materials, which will greatly amuse the amateur in his leisure hours to imitate them, and if he goes by the models, and their descriptions, he will find them, when completed, what may be termed by a Salmon fisher, magnificent. Their life-like and alluring appearance, when humoured attractively with the rod and line, will cause them to be very deceptive to the Salmon, and they will rise out of the water at them with such greediness (the fun of it is) as to mistake them for living insects. I have seen them swim after the fly for some distance, as quietly as possible, before making a rush at it, then seize it, show their back fin, and then the points of their tail—the break of the water they have made closes—you "rise your hand," and the hook is "anchored."

No. 1. I shall name this The Spirit Fly, in consequence of its numerously-jointed body, its fanciful, florid, and delicate appearance. Its colours will be found most enticing to the fish, and is a sister fly to Ondine, in the "Book of the Salmon," by "Ephemera."

The wings are made of six toppings, with a broad strip of wood duck on each side, a red Hymalaya crest feather at top, a cock of the rock feather, blue kingfisher feather at each side, a black head, and feelers of macaw. The body is made of joints of black, orange floss, and a tip of gold tinsel at the tail, tail two small toppings, a tag of puce silk and ostrich, (it must be tied with very fine silk that the body may not be lumpy, but to show gradually taper from the tail to the head, and the hackle to be stripped at one side to roll even), and at each joint a scarlet hackle, with a tip of gold tinsel under each joint, to make it lively looking. There is a purple hackle, or very dark blue, struck round the shoulder. The size of the hook is No. 6 or 7. Salmon, B or BB.

No. 2. The wings are composed of golden pheasant tail feather, mixed with the following: strips of bustard, scarlet macaw, wood-duck, mallard, yellow macaw body feather, silver pheasant, and a topping over all, extending a little longer than the other feathers; blue and yellow macaw feelers. The wing, as above, should be laid out on a piece of paper, ready to tie on after the body and legs are formed, the jay rolled over the head in this fly, and the head tied on last, of black ostrich. The tail is a topping, mixed with a strip of wood-duck feather, tipped with silver twist, a tag of gold-colour floss, and black ostrich; the body puce floss to the centre, and the remainder orange pig hair or mohair, ribbed with broad silver tinsel, and a guinea-hen rump feather rolled over the orange beneath the jay hackle. This is about as fine a specimen of a Salmon fly as ever was thrown into the water, and will kill Salmon and Grilse, made small, in every Salmon river in Great Britain. The hook No. 6 or 9, Limerick.

The best Irish hooks are numbered from No. 1, largest Salmon size, to No. 10, Sea-Trout size.

No. 3. This is another of the Spirit Flies that kill so well in the rivers of Ireland and Scotland, at high water, particularly the Spey and Tweed. The wings are made of the following mixtures of feathers, each side of the wings to be alike: Brown mallard, bustard and wood-duck; a topping, scarlet macaw, teal, golden pheasant neck feather, a strip of yellow macaw, and feelers of blue and yellow tail; a head of black ostrich; the tail to be a topping, mixed with green and red parrot tail; the body is composed of joints, first a tip of silver, a tag of morone floss, a tag of black, a joint of brown, green and brown-red hackle, puce and red, green and yellow, blue and orange, with a tip of gold tinsel at each joint, a very small red hackle, and two red toucan feathers round the shoulder, and blue kingfisher's feather on each side of the wings. The hook No. 6, and No. 10 for Grilse.

No. 4. A celebrated Claret Fly, of very killing qualities both in Scotland and Ireland, and in the Thames as a trout fly. The wings are composed of two wood-duck feathers wanting the white tips, and two strips of the same kind of feather with white tips; the head is made of peacock harl; the tail is two or three strips of hen pheasant tail, with a short tuft of red orange macaw body feather or parrot, tipped with silver, and gold ribbing over the body, which is formed of claret pig hair, over which roll two richly dyed claret hackles, struck in fine proportion from the tail up. The hook No. 6 or 10. It is a capital fly in lakes for large trout, as a breeze or gentle gale only causes a ripple, and a strong wind does not do so well in lakes with the fly, as it makes waves, although good for a large size minnow.

No. 5. A brown fly, a general favorite among the "old ones," on every salmon river in Ireland and Scotland, particularly the latter, and in rivers a good way up from the sea, on a dark day, with a good breeze blowing up the stream. The following fly, No. 6, may be used in a similar manner. The wings are made of the golden pheasant tail that has the long clouded bar in the feather, rather full, and two rather broad strips of light brown white-tipped turkey tail feather at each side; a good size peacock harl head, and feelers of scarlet macaw feather; tipped at the tail with gold tinsel—the tail a small bright topping, and a tag of gold-colour floss silk; the body is made of cinnamon, or yellow-brown pig hair or mohair, ribbed with double silver twist; over the body roll a real brown red cock's hackle, and round the throttle roll on a bright red-brown small-spotted grouse hackle, or a brown mottled feather of the hen Argus pheasant's neck or back. BB hook, or a No. 8.

No. 6. A Silver Grey Fly, a great favorite on the lakes of Killarney for Salmon and Grilse, and at Waterville, in the County of Kerry, for Sea and White Trout, made small on a No. 10 hook, about the size of a No. 6 Trout hook of English make. The wings are made of golden pheasant tail feather, mixed with mallard, red macaw, blue and yellow body feathers of the macaw, guinea hen, and golden pheasant neck feathers, with feelers of blue and yellow macaw, a black head; tipped at the tail with silver and orange floss tag, the tail a topping mixed with red and blue macaw feather, (those blues that are found under the wings of that bird which are of a very light hue) and guinea hen: the body is made of the silver dun monkey if it can be got, light dun fox or squirrel fur, or dyed blue dun mohair mixed with yellow,—all these are good for a body, ribbed with broad silver tinsel, and a hackle of a real dun cock that has a yellowish motley shade throughout it, rolled up to the head, and round the shoulder a bright orange dyed hackle, underneath which tie in a little orange mohair. It may be varied with a claret hackle at the head, or a fiery brown one. No. 9 hook. A small grilse or sea-trout hook, for small rivers in either Scotland or Ireland, and also in the rivers of Wales, where it is a native dun colour among the anglers. It will be found a "don" to rise them.

No. 7. A large dun palmer with a double hook, which, will be observed, is of a tortuous shape in the body, as it appears in the plate. The shape may be obtained by tying the hooks back to back, the top one to be tied about quarter way down the shank of the end one, and the gut tied tightly on each, (twisted gut of course when you form a loop).

It will be found a "killer" in large pools surrounded with trees in stormy weather, and in rapid streams running into or near the sea, where they take it most likely for a shrimp, as it corresponds in color. The legs are composed of about six hackles of a real blue dun old cock-saddle feather, having a motley yellowish hue, and peacock harl head, rather full; the body is made of orange pig hair and yellow mohair mixed, the former drawn out amongst the fibres of the hackles, which must be struck on two at a time, commencing at the tail, till it is all built up to the head, where there may be three hackles to make it fuller,—it would be as well to have a small swivel at the head, that it might spin gently round when moved in the water. No. 9 hook, or small grilse size for large trout. It may be varied with gold, old dun cock's hackles, and red body.

No. 8 is a beautiful specimen of a gaudy fly. The wings, which are finely mixed of rich feathers, are made of the following sorts:—orange, yellow, and blue macaw body feathers, three strips of each; teal, bustard, and golden pheasant neck feathers broken in strips; silver pheasant tail, light brown golden pheasant tail feather, and a topping over all a little longer; a peacock harl head, and blue and yellow feelers. The body is formed in three joints, a tip of gold twist at the tail, a tag of peacock harl, and a bright small topping for tail; first, a joint of yellow floss, a joint of peacock, and two feathers of the red-tipped feather of the crest of the cock of the rock tied short above the harl and ribbed with gold; the next is a blue floss silk joint ribbed with gold, a peacock harl rolled on close, and two feathers of the crest of the cock of the rock tied close above it; and the third is an orange floss silk joint, a peacock harl tag, and ribbed with gold, two of the red-tipped feathers tied on close as above, and a blue jay round the shoulder. No. 8 hook on B. This is a famous grilse fly.

No. 9 is another great beauty, and a capital grilse or small salmon fly for any river under the sun. The wings are made of two jungle-cock feathers, and two shorter feathers of the golden pheasant neck, the white ends of the jungle-cock to show well beyond the golden pheasant neck, two broad strips of wood-duck, one at each side, and a topping or two extending longer than the other feathers for feelers, a black ostrich head; a tip of gold at the tail, a tag of yellow-green silk, a tag of black ostrich, and a bright topping for tail, above the ostrich a blue tag, and the body made of claret floss silk, ribbed with gold tinsel, and claret dyed hackle struck over the body, with a blue jay feather at the shoulder. The hook B or BB.

No. 10. This is a famous high water fly for all salmon rivers, particularly in Scotland, and is not unlike the once celebrated "Parson Fly," the favourite killer in all rivers of the Reverend St. John's; there is no salmon can resist its attractions in rapid pools in rivers near the sea. The preceding fly, No. 9, will be found to kill better a few miles higher up from the sea, as all plain flies do. If the No. 9 is winged with brown mallard or brown turkey tail feather, it will be found just the thing.

The wings are made of two golden pheasant neck feathers, with a broad strip of peacock wing feather on each side, and a strip of scarlet macaw tail feather, the latter to be a little longer than the other feathers, a black ostrich head with a full brilliant blue jay feather round the shoulder. The body is made thus:—a tip of silver twist, a yellow floss silk tag, two small toppings for tail, the body is of golden yellow pig hair or mohair, ribbed with silver twist, with two golden yellow dyed hackles with a black streak up the centre, rolled from the tail to the head. No. 9 hook, B, or BB.

No. 11 is a fly that will kill grilse or salmon in the light running rivers of the North of Scotland, and in all rivers where the salmon and its varieties haunt, and is made of different sizes. The wings are made of a few fibres of each of the following feathers: black and white small spotted bustard rump feather, teal, wood-duck, silver hen pheasant tail, and the silver cock pheasant tail black and white spotted feathers, the neck feather of the golden pheasant, and the red spear feather of the same bird, and at each side two small feathers of the black and white jungle cock, a black head, and topping. The body is made half yellow and half purple pig hair or mohair, the latter colour next the head, over which roll close up two black heron feathers off the crest; a tip of gold, and a small topping for tail, and over the yellow or purple body roll double gold twist. No. 7 hook, or BB.

The Sea-Trout Fly underneath No. 11 in the same plate, will be found a killer either for sea-trout or grilse, in the rivers in Scotland, and the South of Ireland. The wings are made of a dark brown grouse hackle that grows on the rump of the bird, just above the tail, mixed with a small quantity of light brown turkey tail, or kite tail, which is the salmon tail glede of the north, and two feelers of blue and yellow macaw; a black head; the body is made with a tip of silver twist at the tail, and a tag of black ostrich; the tail is a mixture of golden pheasant neck feather, and brown mallard, two or three fibres of each; the body is blue floss silk, rather light, with an old black cock's hackle rolled over it, ribbed with fine silver twist; round the shoulder roll a claret or scarlet hackle. The hook No. 10, or C, double CC, or B, for grilse. There may be three or four varieties of this fly made thus:—body blue, with blue jay, same wings, with a little neck feather of the golden pheasant; orange body, same coloured hackle, and same wings, blue jay at head; a dun body, with fiery brown hackle at the head; a claret body—a yellow body, and small grouse; blue body, and guinea hen; and a yellow body, with guinea hen; a black body, black hackle, and the same wings and tail; a black fly, with teal wings; a brown body, brown hackle, and "glede" wings, two fibres of the same for tail. All these are the choicest colours for sea-trout and grilse flies in every salmon river in the kingdom.

No. 12. Is a large Spring Fly used generally in the Shannon, and the Tweed, when the rivers are very high and rapid. It will be found a mag-

nificent specimen of a gaudy salmon fly, and is the proper size for March and April, when the fulness of the stream prevents the fish from seeing smaller ones. This fly will be seen to perfection in the Plate. With this, I will describe three or four others of the same size, of different colours, which came into my possession from Castle Connell, on the Banks of the Shannon.

The wings of No. 12 are made of the small spotted brown Argus tail feather, golden pheasant tail, and the black and white peacock wing feather; scarlet and blue macaw, and in the centre an orange macaw feather whole, those that are tipped with blue and green—they are found on the shoulders of the red macaw and down the back; a tuft of broken neck feather of the golden pheasant at the head, and feelers of blue and yellow macaw; a black head; a tip of gold at the tail, a tag of blue, another of orange floss and black ostrich, a good sized topping in the tail, and at its root a tuft of red spear feather of the golden pheasant rump; there is about half an inch body at the tail end, made of yellow mohair, and yellow hackle over it, ribbed with gold, the remainder of the body is made of puce floss silk, with a dark wine-purple hackle struck over it, ribbed with silver twist and flat gold, and a yellow body feather of the macaw rolled round the shoulder. The hook, No. 2 or 3, large Salmon size.

SPRING FLIES.

The following fine large flies will be excellent killers in the Shannon, the Tweed, the Thurso, the Spey, and the Tay, in the spring season. The bodies to be made small, the wings large.

No. 1. The body is made of sky blue floss silk, ribbed with broad silver tinsel, tip of silver, and orange tag; a dark blue hackle from the tail up; two toppings in the tail, a large yellow pig hair or mohair head (white seal fur dyed yellow does well), a blue jay round the shoulder; the wings are a large yellow and a large blue feather of the macaw, which grows on the back and under the wings of that bird, two orange macaw feathers an inch shorter on each side of them, two toppings, a mixture of argus, bustard, scarlet and blue macaw, good size strips of each. No. 1 hook, full salmon size.

Blacker's Art of Fly Making, &c.,

No. 2. The body is made of black floss silk, tipped with silver, tag of orange, ribbed with broad silver plate up the body, beside which a claret hackle, and the tail two toppings; the wings are made of a large red rump spear feather of the golden pheasant in the centre, four large toppings with a mixture of sprigging at each side of the following: Argus pheasant tail, bustard, blue and yellow macaw, blue jay at the shoulder, and a large size head of puce pig hair. Hook No. 1 or 2, Spring Salmon size.

No. 3. The body is made of black floss silk, ribbed with silver, orange tag, tip of silver, tail a topping with a little red; the wings are made of the whole yellow feathers of the macaw which grow under the wings of the bird, two tipped feathers mixed with bustard, Argus, blue and scarlet macaw, and a blue head of pig hair or mohair. No. 1 or 2 hook.

No. 4. The body is made of light puce floss silk, ribbed with silver plate and gold twist, a claret hackle over it, tipped with silver, a topping for tail, and orange tag; the wings are made of yellow macaw, a red spear feather, four toppings, a mixture of bustard golden pheasant tail, kingfisher's each side, and a large blue head of mohair. (It cannot be too large for the Shannon). No. 1 hook, large Salmon size.

No. 5. The body is made of puce floss, ribbed with broad silver and gold twist, purple hackle over it, orange tag, tip of silver, and tail a topping; the wings are made of two body feathers of the yellow macaw, mixed with blue macaw tail and Argus, two large toppings, and a dark blue pig hair head. Salmon hook No. 2, spring size.

No. 6. This is another excellent fly. The wings are like the last named fly; a black floss body, ribbed with silver, and yellow hackle over it; a large blue head, picked out to hang down like a hackle. No. 3 hook. This is a fly of "The Ogormans," of Ennis, in the County of Clare, see his Work on Angling. The two Salmon Flies in the plate, with "picker," are described for Killarney.

SALMON RIVERS.

It will be most advantageous to my readers that I should give them some accurate accounts of the various Salmon Rivers, pointing out at the same time the best station on each where sport may be expected with the fly, and to know where to proceed before starting on their angling excursion, as the whole fun is in knowing the right places to prevent disap-disappointment. There are numerous small size rivers, the local flies for which are of a plain and sombre hue, and which it will be necessary the fisher should be acquainted with—these I will give as I proceed.

In summer, when the rivers are low, small plain flies are best, or rather so on dark days, with a good ripple, then they will entice them. They do not rise often when the sun is warm, except in rapid streams. Use small black bodied flies with silver and middling gaudy wings, mixed with teal or cock of the north feather—change it to a gaudy one if they do not take the black. Early in the mornings before the sun strikes the water, and from three o'clock till dark, or about sunset is a good time to move a large fish with a fly he likes. The two flies at the bottom of the plate with "picker," are most likely ones for that time in the day. The plain one is brown body, and wings of mallard. The bottom one is green body, and mixed wings of gaudy feathers; the body is a jointed one, of peacock green. I made it nearly twenty years ago,—it is a beautiful specimen of a gaudy fly for rapids after a flood.

THE RIVER TWEED.

I will begin with this large and beautiful salmon river, which runs rapidly along the borders of England and Scotland, taking a course from West to East. It flows majestically through a highly picturesque and cultivated country, washing many good towns on its way to the sea, where it discharges its valuable waters at Berwick.

The town of Kelso is the best station, as there is good fishing above and below it. There is a magnificent spot for a month or more of salmon fishing at a place called "The Throughs," three miles above the town,—it is a real picture of a place to the eyes of the fisher. Higher up is St. Boswell's, and a little higher, Melrose—both charming places. There is good angling in the Tiviot, at Kelso, in the spring; it runs into the Tweed on the opposite side. The trout are numerous in it. There are several capital stations below the town, where the fish take the fly most freely, which is not the case in most of the rivers of the same magnitude. The fifteen painted salmon flies will be found excellent killers in this noble river, and the six large spring flies.

I have killed Grilse, Sea-Trout, and River-Trout with the Winged Larva at the "Throughs" in August. Easterly winds were prevailing at the time, and the fish would not stir at any other sort of fly. When the river runs very low small flies are best.

THE RIVER SHANNON.

This is the largest and finest Salmon river in Britain. There is not a river in Norway that can be compared to it for fishing, were it properly used. The angler must proceed to its banks before he can say, conscientiously, that he has ever seen a salmon river. In its course it expands into three large and beautiful lakes, Lough Allen, Lough Ree, and Lough Derg. There are numerous islands in the latter one, with ruins of religious edifices, &c. This noble river receives many tributaries, in which there is capital fly fishing, with rapids and falls of water till it reaches Limerick. It runs a hundred and twenty miles to this place, and sixty more to the sea. It is on leaving the lakes that it abounds with many delightful streams—the haunts of large Salmon and fine Trout. Six miles above Limerick, at Castle Connel, there is a splendid place for the fly, and Trout fishing is good. The angler will here behold a scene that will greatly amuse him.

There are other capital casts for Salmon up to Killaloe, where the Pike and Eels are of an extraordinary size and quality. Lough Derg is close to this place, in which are caught the "Gillaroe" Trout; they have gizzards like turkeys, are short and round in the body, very red in the flesh when cooked, and they have a most delicious flavour.

The best flies for the Shannon are the fifteen painted ones, and the six large flies for spring. You cannot fail with these beautiful flies.

THE LAKES OF CLARE.

From the town of Killaloe the angler may proceed to the lakes of the County of Clare. You go west to the town of Broadford, eight miles distant, where there are three or four lakes, the furthest off one, Dromore; this town is eighteen miles off, and about eight from the county town, Ennis, on the river Fergus. Twelve miles up this river is Corrafin, a neat town, near which is the celebrated lake of "Inchiquin," famous for its large trout and splendid views. Here the angler will find boats and every accommodation.

The flies in my list for the season will kill exceedingly well in these lakes, made two or three sizes larger, and in fine weather the size they are.

They are fond of grouse hackle, wrens, browns, turf-coloured flies, amber, black, grey, &c., &c., with brown grouse wings. The "yarn fly"[2] is not used here.

Before the tourist angler leaves Killaloe, if he has time, he should by all means see the antiquities of the place, Lough Derg and Holy Island, where there are to be seen the ruins of seven churches, and a round tower 70 feet high, the entrenchments of "Brian Boroimhe," King of Munster, at Cancora, and his tomb near the Cathedral in the town.

This ancient town is seated on the western bank of the Shannon, in the County of Clare, over which there is a bridge of nineteen arches; at a short distance below it, this grand river rolls over tremendous ledges of rocks, where there is an excellent fishery. It is a great pity that this fine river should be prevented from being of the greatest benefit to the country through which it runs, all owing to the "cruives," the "stake nets," "bag nets," and every other destructive invention that can be contrived for the wholesale slaughter of the splendid Salmon. Oh! look to it, you that have the power.

---

[2] **FOOTNOTE:** Net.

From Limerick the angler may proceed to Athlone and Galway, but I should advise him to proceed to the south first, and fish the Blackwater and the lakes of Killarney; Mr. Jas. Butler has prohibited the fishing at Waterville this spring, in consequence, as he says, "of the numbers visiting, coupled with acts of poaching." I should say the lake is free, as it always was and ever has been, knowing that Mr. Butler is most polite to gentlemen.

THE LAKES OF KILLARNEY.

From Mallow, on the Blackwater, the angler proceeds to Killarney. It would be as well to go to Lismore, farther down from Mallow, where there is good Salmon fishing to be had; there is a Mr. Foley here (who rents the "weirs" of the Duke of Devonshire), he is most polite to strangers, and allows them to fish in the weirs, which are of some extent; and most of the Gentlemen residing on its banks, from Lismore up, will allow the stranger to fly-fish through their grounds, send their keepers to shew them the best places, and are most hospitable and polite. At the Killarney junction, Mallow, the angler takes his seat, and in a little time is delighted with the sight of the Lakes. I visited Killarney in 1848, on an angling excursion in Ireland, to recruit my fallen spirits, if possible, after many years of industrious labour, "and it is myself that would advise the sickly to go there, if he had legs to walk on," says poor Pat.

To my great disappointment at the time, the Lakes were netted by their respective owners, which rather damped my spirits after going so far "a fishing"—my sport there was but inferior. It is not so now, many thanks to Lord Kenmare and Mr. Herbert, who have put a stop to the netting and other contrivances, to the delight of the anglers and inn keepers of the neighbourhood. I have been given to understand that the Salmon fishing is capital now in the lakes and river. At Ennisfallen Island there is a favourite cast, and another between that and Ross Island; another to the south west of it; towards Mucruss Abbey, to the north-east, there is good water for the fly, and in "Glena" bay, all of which the boatmen will show. At the latter place parties dine, in a very beautiful situation at the foot of the hill, sheltered by trees to the water's edge. On the west side of it is shown a curiosity—a holly, a thorn, a birch, a hazel, an ash, and an oak, so curiously entwined, that they appear as one tree; at this place there is a good fishery, at the cottage they cut the salmon into pieces, skewer them with arbutus, and roast them over a turf fire; they say arbutus gives them a fine flavour.

Between Brickeen Bridge and the Upper Lake there is good fishing, in the narrow gorge between the lakes; the charges of boats, &c., have been regulated, so that they cannot now impose upon visitors. The scenery in the vicinity of "Brickeen Bridge" and the Eagle's Nest is sublime, and must delight the heart of the Angler who may be seeking health and pastime, either by himself or with his dear admiring friends.

There is not a table, either in inn or lodging house in the town of Killarney, wanting a Guide to the Lakes, written by some intelligent person or other, so that the angler cannot go astray.

There are numerous good inns in the town and neighbourhood, the people and landlords of which are polite, civil, and obliging to strangers, as are the guides and boatmen.

There is a Miss Smith, in New Street, who keeps a comfortable lodging, the most honest creature I ever came across, go to her, you gentle ones.

The delightful Island of Ennisfallen, which used to be my favourite spot during my stay, would be a kind of Heaven on Earth to the invalid; it is covered with verdure and beautiful large trees, the arbutus, &c. There is a thorn growing through a tomb stone, a holly fourteen feet thick, a curious crab tree, and the bed of honour, which the guides say if you lie down in it, having no children up to the present time, "your honor will be sure to have plenty of them after your return home."—This place is a hollow about the size of a large bed, in a projecting rock overhung with holly and hawthorn. In an aperture in the "crab tree" the guides recommend ladies to pass. There are ruins of a once celebrated Abbey here, founded in an early date of St. Finian.

The annals of Ennisfallen comprise a history of the world up to a.d. 430, and a history of Ireland up to 1320. They are preserved in Trinity College, Dublin. There is an enormous ash tree growing out of the floor of the abbey. It is unquestionably a healthy spot, and soon excites an appetite by inhaling its salubrious air.

The remains of the once beautiful edifice "Mucruss Abbey" is well worth seeing, as the ravages of death, which were once too prominent, have been cleared away by the humane Mr. Herbert, so that there may be a close inspection made of the ruins; the architecture of the eastern window is admirable; and the extraordinary "yew tree" growing in the centre of the ancient cloisters and over-spreading its walls is curious in the extreme, in the fork of the yew, above the great trunk, there is a kind of unctuous gum constantly flowing down, which is said by the peasantry that "the yew is shedding tears for the fate of the abbey."

The Salmon flies to suit the Lakes, are Nos. 2, 4, 5, and 6, 8 and 9 the two at the bottom of the plate with "picker," and No. 4 plate on Salmon hooks, the paintings of which are exact to the models. The three latter flies are, first, a cinnamon-brown body, brown wings, and brown red hackle, mixed tail; second, a jointed body fly of blue and green, gaudy mixed wing, topping in the tail—this fly may be used in very rough water, and the brown one with a nice ripple and grey cloud; the No. 4 fly on Salmon hooks, is mallard wings, fiery brown body ribbed with gold, brown red hackle, hook No. 6, B, CC, and a yellow and red mixed tail. The Dun Salmon Fly, No 6, and the one above it, No 5, are favourite killers in the lakes and river.

My advise is, that my friends (I call every angler who reads this book a friend), should beware of the "mountain dew"[3] and goat's milk, sold by the damsels of Killarney, in the vicinity of Brickeen Bridge, and the Eagle's nest; they are harmless and cleanly creatures, but their importunity to taste their goat's milk is teasing—buy their goat's milk, but reject their "dew," gentle fishers.

The river "Lane," which issues out of the Lower Lake, as it is now preserved by the inn keepers, is a capital stream for salmon and sea trout fishing; about four miles from Killarney, at the Bridge leading to "Dunloe Gap," is a good place to begin to fish, either up or down the river; the trout in both lakes and river are as yellow as gold when taken out of the

---

[3] **FOOTNOTE:** Whiskey—Oh! whiskey, whiskey,—cruel whiskey, you are the cause of poor Pat's giant poverty, you have rushed in upon him like one armed. Oh! thou accursed evil spirit.

water, they are spotted over with beautiful brown-red marks, and are very handsome to look at.

The Trout Flies in the list will be found excellent for the lakes and river. A grouse hackle, with orange silk body, and a little strip of grey partridge tail for wings—this with the ant brown, hare's ear, and amber fly; the red dun, caperer, wren and cuckoo hackle, and duns of various shades and size, ribbed with silver. The land-rail fly, brown-red hackle, and ash fox, an orange body with black hackle from the tail up, and starling wings. The silver dun, with grey mallard wings, mixed with the wing of the bunting lark, ribbed with silver, and tail of the hackle fibres, the body yellow dun—this is a great favourite made of sea-trout size for the river, and large for salmon in the lakes. The sand and cinnamon flies are also good, and the red spinner; the winged larva is an excellent fly below the Bridge, allowed to sink a little beneath the surface when fished with, grilse and sea-trout will take it.

The river Lane is remarkable for its firm footing along the banks, and no where obstructed by trees, it is the most pleasant place I ever saw for fishing, combined with wild and fanciful scenery.

LOUGH CURRAN, WATERVILLE.

The angler may proceed any morning he feels disposed, to Waterville river and lake, southwest of Killarney, in the County Kerry; there is a car from the Kenmare Arms Hotel about eight o'clock in the morning, passing through Killorglan at the foot of the river Lane, which you have in view up to this place; Three miles farther on you come to the river "Corra," where there is an Inn, at the Bridge, for the accommodation of anglers, and where they may procure capital sea-trout and small grilse fishing; the lake Carra, out of which the river flows, is seen to the left before reaching the river at the bridge. It would be worth while staying a few days at this place, as the sea-trout fishing is beyond comparison, be low the bridge to the sea, and above it as far as the lake, and also in the lake. The flies I have just named will kill well in the Carra, with a small black one, like a midge, ribbed with silver, with a honey dun fly made very small.

You reach "Cahirceveen" in about eight hours from Killarney, from whence you take a car eight miles further on to Waterville, where you arrive comfortably in the evening to rest and have a talk with Mr. Butler, the proprietor of the "cuts;" the angler will find him most civil and polite, and on asking you get instant permission to angle for salmon in the river, and "keep all you catch" which has been a general rule for a length of time; the lake is free for salmon and trout fishing, it abounds with fine sea-trout, which appear to be continually running up between the bars of the "cruives." The river is very small, having but one pool in it close to the sea for salmon, the run of it is very short as the lake and sea almost meet, they are separated merely by a neck of land on which the bridge and "cuts" are erected, about three or four perches altogether. There is good sport to be had in the lake and river when it is flooded, and the angler will find every convenience with respect to men and boats; there are two inns in the place, at least when I was there in 1848, there were two.

The flies for Waterville are the same as those I have just given, except for salmon in the river, which should be very plain and sombre, they are brown bodies, with dark hackles over a roll or two of gold tinsel, and brown turkey wings of a reddish hue; small blue flies, with gaudy wings, ribbed with silver, and black heads, the hackle to be dyed blue, and floss silk body, hook No. 10 or C. CC. When the water is up they will take Nos. 3, 4, and 5 flies in the plates; and the fly No. 11 is most excellent. They use a good sized fly in the lake for trout, when I fished it my flies were of the smaller sort, and in the hot sun the trout took small amber flies best with me. The local flies were darker—say drake size, with brown bodies, black hackles, and turkey wings, nevertheless they take them in a windy day exceedingly quick, and in a very short time the fishermen in the boats catch a large dish of them, say in about a hour; the trout and grilse in this lake I must say are most delicious, "they almost melt in the mouth," says he.

The angler, when he gets tired here, may return to Killarney, and make head for the west and north, "and sure enough he may have another throw on the lakes, if he pleases, by way of bidding them good bye."

He might take a start before he goes across the hills to Kenmare, by car, and have a day or two on the river Blackwater, usually called "Kerry Blackwater;" it is about eight miles from Kenmare, on the south-west side of the estuary of that name, on the road to "Derrynane Beg," or Derrynane Abbey. There is an inn on the river as you cross the road, but no town. The angler might go to it for a day or so from Waterville, by hiring a car at the inn, there and back. He will have an opportunity of seeing the mansion of the late Mr. D. O'Connell, at Derrynane, as he passes it to his right off the road, in a most healthy situation, sequestered amongst dwarf trees of the most fanciful appearance, close to a bay of the sea, or what is called "Kenmare River," the salt water of which is as clear as crystal.

The flies used on this prolific little river are brown bodies, three ribs of gold tinsel, black hackles, and grouse and mallard wings; but I would strongly advise the angler to have some of the small flies made smaller still for this river, than in the plates of flies. A very small blue jay, a silver grey or "hedgehog fly," with a small black one ribbed with silver, are all good for this stream.

The angler returns to old Killarney, and takes rail for Limerick, from thence by steam to Athlone, on the "Great Western;" there are fine Trout and Salmon here in summer. Go on from here to Galway, and fly fish Lough Carib (the river, I believe, is now broken up to facilitate the navigation between the bay and this grand expanse of fresh water). There are very large Trout to be met with in the Lough, and every accommodation respecting fishermen and boats at the town. The angler will find it very pleasant for a day or two's fish in the lake, with a ripple on the water and a grey cloud above.

CONNAMARA AND BALLYNAHINCH.

In this western region there are some beautiful lakes and rivers, once celebrated for the abundance of Salmon and Trout which they contained, but, alas! the "weirs" and nets have "wed" them all away, to the grief of the tourist angler, who might have enjoyed the "wild sports of the west." So he will yet, for there is a reformation to take place that will restore them to their pristine numbers both in lake and river. They are about to take down the "weirs," and net the bays, which will not only give the Salmon a free passage up, but augment them a hundred-fold,— then, "hurrah for Connamara, the land of the west." Derry Clare Lake is a good one for the fly, so is Lough Inna, and above and below the "weirs." If the generous proprietors of the fishery would consult upon the subject, they would immediately put a stop to the obstructions, if not, it it is quite impossible that there can be good fishing up to Lough Inna. Thirty gentlemen might fly fish these waters without the least inconvenience, were the Salmon allowed to go free.

The Salmon Flies for Connamara are rather small and plain; various brown, black, red, olive, and orange flies kill well, ribbed with gold and silver. Those Sea-Trout ones, described for Waterville, do also well, and orange floss silk, ribbed with gold, small topping for tail, jay round the head, and mallard mixed wings. Hook C or CC.

A small black fly, yellow tag, topping for tail, rib of silver, teal, and golden pheasant neck, breast feather of the peacock wing, mixed, blue feelers of macaw, jay at the shoulder. Hook B, or No. 9. A green body, ribbed with gold, black red hackle, orange macaw, or cock of the rock feather in the tail, short; a nice mixed gaudy wing, with a good deal of mallard and wood-duck prevailing, or silver pheasant wing, the hen bird is best. C, CC or B hook; vary the size for high and low water. A small claret fly, and the three flies in the Plates, Nos. 3, 4, and 5, with No. 11, all made on small hooks, these are the sorts to kill. The Sea-Trout ones are very small black and red hackles, grouse and wren hackles, dun flies, and little brown ants, hare's ear and yellow, silver greys, and the small flies enumerated in the catalogue. Use a sixteen feet salmon rod, and single gut casting lines, with one or two twisted lengths next to the reel line, which should be plaited silk and hair. There are plenty of boats and boatmen to be had at Ballynahinch River and Lakes, all civil fellows, and if used with common kindness and decency, they will confess that "the English anglers are the best fellows in the whole world,—Good luck to their honors. Long life to their honors."

The scenery of this wild country is quite equal to any in Scotland, if the intelligent tourist angler would be at the pains of penetrating into the mountainous regions which surround Connamara. The islands in the bays are interesting and beautiful, as well as the stupendous hills standing up in order like giants, as it were, to bid defiance to the wild waves of the great Atlantic.

Ireland is proverbial for the finest breeding rivers in the world for Salmon and Trout, in no country can there be found such splendid rivers and lakes for Salmon; see, for instance, the rivers Shannon, Erin, Bann, and the stupendous lakes out of which they issue, and of which, it is sufficient to show, that at "Burn Cranna," two miles below Coleraine, with the cross nets, three tons of Salmon were caught in one day by the fishermen some years back. This will give an idea of what the rivers in Ireland, in general, can produce. The Bann is preserved in the right season for the fry to come to perfection in great shoals, and from March till August the nets and "cruives" are worked.

The flavour and quality of the Irish Salmon far exceed those of any other part of the United Kingdom, for when the fish are sent up from the north to the London markets they often lose their flavour, if not properly packed in the ice boxes; how can it be otherwise, when the distance is considered. The real Salmon of the Tweed, Tay, and Spay, are delicious, through the quickness of transit.

Above Ballynahinch are seen the "Twelve Pins," or rocky precipices of "Beanabola." On the right of this mountainous road, beyond Ballynahinch, opposite the beautiful island of "Ennisbofine," are seen green mountain heights of great elevation, with romantic winding vallies, rivers, and views, that strike the heart with admiration.

There is a large river in this neighbourhood, called the "Owen Rieve," which abounds with Salmon, and falls into the sea south of Clue Bay. At the head of the Bay, a short way up, there is a Salmon Fishery, but no inn.

BALLYNA.

The angler may now proceed to the river Moy, at Ballyna, in the County of Mayo, a celebrated place for ages for Salmon fishing with the fly, and also a place where he may find every facility for insuring sport by the kind and obliging conduct of the renter of the "cruives," or cuts, who politely allows the angler to fish where he pleases, on condition that he gives up his fish save one per day, which he may freely reserve for himself, and as a trophy of his success, have the honor of "cutting it pink" by a good turf fire, tired after the day's sport, washing it down with a smoking hot tumbler of "whiskey punch," drinking the health of the Queen, and success to the arms of our brave countrymen in the East.

Lough Con will be found also good, but the trout fishing is best in it—fly fish the river for salmon. It is about ten miles up to the southwest, and in it may be caught with the fly, the gilla-roe trout that have gizzards, the same as in Lough Derg on the Shannon. From the town of Ballyna up to Foxford, eight miles distant, is all capital water for salmon; there are plenty of boats to be had, and those who do not like a boat may fish from the shore; the salmon will rise and take the fly in every part of this water, so that the angler cannot go astray.

The flies in use here are rather plain than gaudy, except in the spring, like all other rivers, they must be larger and more of a gaudy hue.

A claret body, claret hackle and gold rib, tail a small topping, an orange tag rather tapered to the shoulder, jay at head, mallard wings mixed with blue and yellow macaw, neck feather of the golden pheasant, a topping over all, guinea hen, teal, and blue macaw feelers each side with a kingfisher, hook CC, 9, or BB.

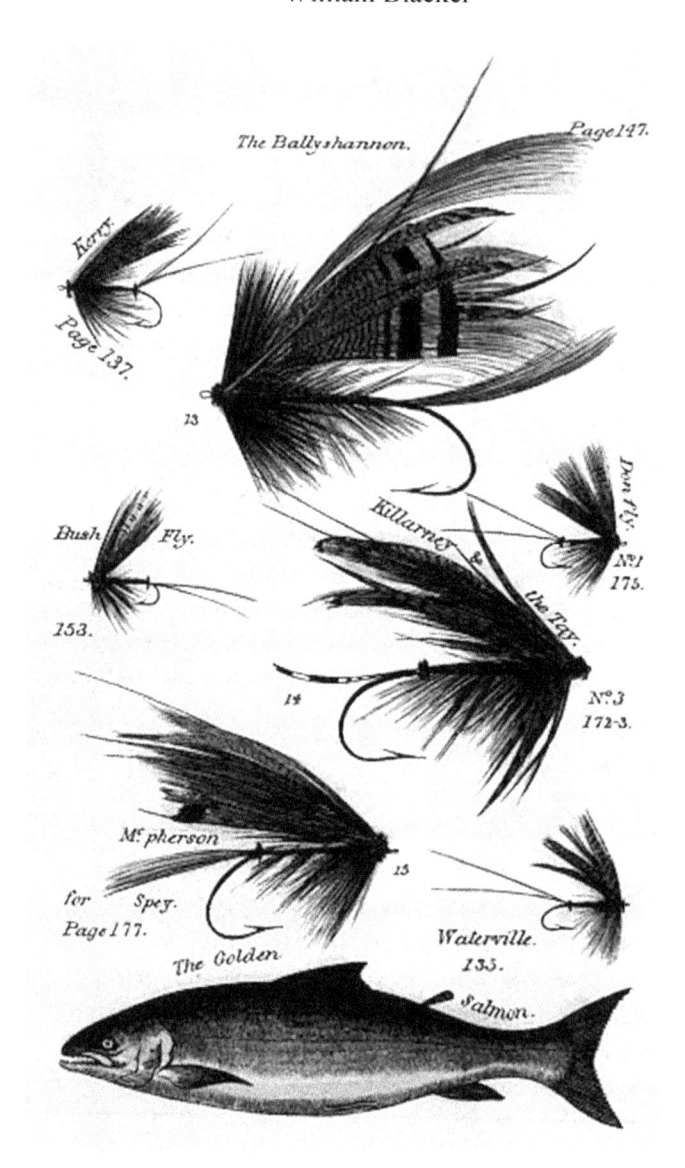

A fly, with a fiery brown floss silk body, black ostrich tag, hackle of the same colour as body, rib of gold, tail of topping, mallard, golden pheasant tail, neck, and red rump feathers mixed, a blue jay or small guinea hen feather at the shoulder, hook No. 9, or B in low water.

A blue body, blue jay over it, tag of orange floss, topping for tail, the hackle to be made full by another jay at the shoulder, under which roll a piece of orange pig-hair and pick it out well through the jay; the wings to be mixed ones with a topping in the centre; scarlet macaw feelers, and black head; hook No. 9 and B; rib the body with silver tinsel, and let it be the same colour as the jay.

These with Nos. 1, 3, 4, and 5, in the plates of flies for salmon will be found excellent. No. 11 is a good one; and a fly made with black silk body ribbed with silver twist, a very small topping in the tail, mixed with a sprig or two of guinea hen and Ibis, a small guinea hen hackle over the body and cut slantingly underneath the body to be longer at the shoulder, and a black or peacock head with a small blue jay round it; wings mixed with dark mallard, teal, neck feather, blue and yellow macaw, and a strip or two of wood-duck each side, and a fibre or two of peacock neck and white spotted wing feather, hook CC, B. If these flies are attended to, they will kill when many others fail; do not lose your sport and time, keep to what I say.

BALLYSHANNON.

From Ballyna the angler may proceed to the Erne, at Ballyshannon, by coach, where he will find, on his arrival, a beautiful river, and every accommodation he requires; it is a short running river, with a deep and rapid current, about three or four miles in length; at the town of Bellick it flows out of the grand expanse of Lough Erne, fifty miles in length, and in some parts twelve in width.

The salmon leap of Ballyshannon, is a broad body of water falling over a perpendicular rock twelve feet high, up which the salmon run, showing their dark backs through the foaming water, and again falling back into the pool below after many attempts to surmount it; they seldom leap clean up out of the water, but in general I have seen them rushing up through the falling current, which shows the extraordinary strength they possess. I have remarked that they always remain a day or two in the first pool they come to after their ascent, and in this they take the fly most greedily, generally at the head of the leap.

The fishermen sweep the river with nets below the leap, and the enormous quantities they take is most surprising, still there is abundance in the river; in summer in consequence of the netting, of course the salmon are not so plentiful up the river. The fish house stands on an island, which may be seen from the bridge of fourteen arches, and in the distance the sea views are grand.

There is capital fishing below the bridge, and many fine salmon throws or haunts all the way up to Belleek; this town is finely situated on the north of Lough Erne, where it begins to discharge its waters into the channel which conveys them into the bay of Donnegal.

The river at this place has a fall of twenty feet, forming a beautiful scene, enriched by foliage and steep precipices. The trout fishing here is good.

The river Erne has a long course, the source of which is "Lough Gonnagh," in the County Longford, a short way from "Lough Sheelin," and the celebrated Lakes of West Meath. It then enters "Lough Oughter," in the County Cavan, after a serpentine course of eighteen or twenty miles, although the distance between the lakes is only eight miles; after passing through this lake, it takes another winding course of the same distance, passing Belturbet, an ancient town on its banks, it then enters the upper Lough Erne, and falls into the sea at Ballyshannon. Seeing the abundance of fish which these grand lakes, and clear running streams throughout the country produce, it is not at all to be wondered at the quantities taken at Ballyshannon.

The flies in use here are very gaudy, Nos. 1, 2, and 3, in the plates, will be found capital killers, and up to No. 11 in fine days in summer when the water is low.

There is another good killer which I will here describe:—body yellow brown mohair, ribbed with silver twist, puce tag, topping for tail with a little scarlet ibis mixed, a good dyed yellow hackle rolled over the body, and a scarlet hackle round the head; the wings are four toppings with strips of summer duck, a sprig or two of pheasant tail and neck, a strip of dyed white tipped turkey tail, and a sprig of guinea hen and glede or kite tail, the tail feather of the hen Hymalean pheasant is as good as what is called in Scotland "salmon tail glede," and the topping or crest of the cock bird which is a transparent scarlet colour, and like a topping of the golden pheasant stands over all; blue kingfisher each side, and scarlet macaw feelers, black ostrich head, hook No. 9 or 8 in high water. This is a magnificent specimen of a salmon fly, and cannot be made properly at a small expense, either by the amateur himself who buys his foreign feathers, or by the fly-maker who gets his bread by it. The three flies in the plates Nos. 1, 2, and 3, will be found to do the work well. With this one, see the gaudy jointed fly in the plate, with "picker" at top.

THE RIVERS BUSH AND BANN.

From Ballyshannon the angler proceeds to the Enniskillen and Derry railway, where he takes his seat for Coleraine; on arriving at this town he need not expect much fishing, except that he may take a throw at the head of the leap, and take also a view of that stupendous fall of fresh water which there can be little doubt of its surprising him, with the grand and delightful scenes around. When he gets on the suspension bridge, over the very top of the leap, he must hold by the rails to steady himself, and consider where he really is; the noise which the great body of water in the centre fall makes, when it descends into the pool beneath, dins his very ears, this with the broad rapid running river close beneath his feet as he stands on the light iron bridge, holding by a single rail with his hand, must almost take his sight away; and if he never had the pleasure of seeing the shadow of fear before, rely upon it he feels himself in a fearful plight just then "for a short time any how."

On the County Derry side the falls are not so strong, and on these the "cuts" are erected, for no salmon could surmount the centre fall, and these "cuts" are so high from the top of the leap, that the salmon cannot get over them even in floods, except by mere chance. This productive fishery belongs to the London Fishmongers' Company, on application the stranger will be allowed on the bridge to view the falls, and at the same time he will see the traps crowded with salmon of all sizes, from the small "graul," as they call them there, to the largest size salmon; sometimes the fish can hardly swim in these "cuts" or "cruives" they are so numerous, what a treat for the eyes of the fly fisher to behold. The angler may fly fish at will, and has his choice either to go up the Bann to Kilrea, or go first to the Bush river, it is only seven miles from Coleraine to Bush Mills, so that as he is now in that town it would be advisable to try his hand at the Bush first, and then proceed to Kilrea, on the Bann, about fourteen miles up that river, by car.

When the angler arrives at Bush Mills, which he will do in an hour from Coleraine, the inn keeper will make him acquainted with the rules of the fishing. The river is now in possession of a club of gentlemen, who will with great pleasure allow the stranger to fly fish.

It will be necessary to have a guide, who will show you all the best throws for salmon; and when tired of fishing, point out the "Causeway" to you, which is two miles from the town. The best of the fishing extends about two miles—one mile below the town to the sea, and one mile above it at the salmon leap.

There are some good throws on the top of the leap, and towards the tail of the large pool beneath; another famous throw between that and the town called "Lagan Drade;" at the top of this long pool there are two large stones projecting out of the water, between which the current of the stream rushes violently, in this rapid place between the stones the fish will take the fly, and below the stones along the left side of the Bush, and on the rising ground at the foot of the pool; if you can manage to throw well over the bushes you will be very apt to hook a salmon in the mid-water. There is another good throw below the bridge; the deepest part lying along the gardens, and three or four more between that and the sea; there is a large stone lies in the middle of the river, over which the water may be seen boiling, if you can manage to throw beyond it, and draw the fly across it letting it fall a little below it, you will have a chance to hook a fish immediately. Just below this stone, a little way from the sea, at a narrow part of the river, is another capital place, fish it from the right side and do not come abruptly upon the place or the fish will see you, which will prevent them from rising, but this you can avoid, as you will see this contracted part from the stone throw; prepare a good fly before you come up, and keep as far off it as possible. It is a shelving elbow shaped rock narrowing the river, so that your fly must be gradually moved down commencing a few yards above the elbow rock, which cannot be seen as the grass grows on it to the very edge, till you look over it into the water; just as the fly rounds the point all the fish see it that are lying under the brow of the hollow rock, where you may expect a rise; this is the deepest part of the whole river, and the first resting place for the fish after leaving the sea.

In this place the depth of the water requires a bright fly; the following one will prove a killer:—Body, orange floss silk, a small topping for tail with a fibre or two of mallard, ribbed with fine gold tinsel, and a rich brown-red cock's hackle from the tail up, not too long in the fibres, the hackle to be a little black at the head when rolled on; the wing of copper brown mallard with a strip of wood-duck each side, and a topping over all; feelers of macaw, and a black ostrich head. Hook CC. Should you rise a fish with this old favorite, and it does not take, try him once or twice more with it, and no doubt you will have him. If he does not hook himself with it, change it for a light blue one, the body the blue colour of the sky, legs the same, and a mallard wing ribbed with gold.

You now come to the sea, at "Bushfoot." There is a pool here into which the tide ebbs and flows, and at times the fish are plunging over and over on the top of each other, which the fishermen net when this is the case. When the tide is out the Salmon will rise and take the fly in it freely, as the flowing of the river into it pushes out the brackish water before it, and when the tide is flowing, before it enters the pool, is the best time,—in fact, this is the best place to stay at for the sole purpose of being enabled to fish, as the river above is so low in summer, except after rains, that it is useless to try.

The Castle of old "Dunluce" is near Bushfoot, it stands on a rock close to the cliff on the mainland in the sea, and is built on the surface or top of the rock, close to its very edge all round, and the corner stones appear to have been brought from the Giant's Causeway. There is a deep chasm between the castle and the land, over which the range wall of the old bridge is yet standing; the bridge itself is completely gone. This narrow wall, about fourteen inches wide, may be easily crossed going into the castle, but on recrossing it to the land side it strikes terror into the heart. Some years ago I visited this old ruin, and crossed the wall into it quite easily and fearlessly, but on my returning, to my great surprise, I was afraid of my life to recross it. The cause was, no doubt, that the wall and yawning chasm appeared more under me on coming out than on going in, the wall being narrow and the chasm deep. At last I crept over it very slowly on my hands and knees, and it was with difficulty I reached the land. As I sat panting on the grass, looking towards the dark old pile, I vowed that the walls of "Dunluce Castle" should never again hold me. I was most likely stricken with a fairy talisman.

The "Giant's Causeway" is two miles from Bushfoot, where the stranger may spend a few pleasant days with a kind friend, amidst rocks and caves, glens and tremendous cliffs, causeways, chasms, and pillars of wondrous height. These rows of pillars stand up the face of the cliff, which is 360 feet high, from the base of which three broad causeways extend, of honeycomb shape, nine hundred feet into the sea. The pillars of these low causeways are generally six, seven, and many three and nine-sided, and as even as if they had been cut with a chisel; they rest one upon another in joints, the top one round to fit into the one beneath like a socket, and the pillars are so closely packed, that you can hardly get the point of a knife between them. There are other pillars in the face of the cliffs, called the Giant's Loom, the Giant's Chair, the Giant's Organ, and the Giant's Well. The natural wildness and grandeur of these and the adjoining promontories, exceed any thing that can be imagined.

THE RIVER BANN.

Portna is considered the best ford for Salmon and Trout fishing on this noble stream. At this place, which is merely an inn, kept by a Mr. Moore, for the accommodation of anglers, the river, which is a large one, falls over ledges of rock, large stones, broad fords of gravel, deep gorges in places, rushing down inclined plains, which spread into currents five and six feet deep, dimpling as it flows along, where large trout may be seen taking down the natural insects, and making the surface boil. These places might be swarming, were it not for the "cruives," with the largest salmon in Britain.

During the summer months you may take a good many salmon here, but on some days you cannot see a fish, as they are mostly stopped at the "cuts." These salmon traps are called "cuts," in Ireland, and "cruives," in Scotland. I need not explain their formation, as they are too well known to the fly fishers. Notwithstanding all this, the generous renter of the fishery at the Leap of Coleraine, gives liberty to all anglers visiting the Bann, from March to August, and the courtesy and politeness which he evinces towards gentlemen, causes him to take no notice of their fishing with the salmon fly till September. I have been informed by Mr. Moore, the inn-keeper, at Portna, that there is now a "Queen's Gap" made in the "cuts," on Sundays, to allow some of the salmon to escape. This is a great boon to the angler.

The town of Kilrea is a mile from Portna, where there is a good inn, kept by an Englishman, a Mr. Adcock. At the bridge, which is half a mile from the town, there is a famous throw for a salmon; you let off the line, while standing on the bridge, to where the fish lie, a little lower down. There are capital streams for salmon near "Moor Lodge," a delightful spot, down as far as "Bevanaher" ford. The boatmen take you through the gorges in racehorse style. The man brings the bow of the boat to the very edge of the rapid, steadies her by making you sit down with himself, and in a minute or two she shoots down the gorge in a very pleasant manner into the broad ford below; when he returns with the boat, he pulls her up the side of the stream. The Bann boatmen, I must say, are very civil fellows, and charge moderately for their labour and boats—half-a-crown a day, pot luck, and a smoke of tobacco—"an ould fly, and a gut casting line, if it's no use to your honor."

The Flies to suit the Bann are as follows:—

No. 1. Body claret pig hair, ribbed with gold tinsel, orange tag, a topping, and a little wood-duck for tail; a dark claret hackle rolled up to the shoulder, and a blue jay above it; mallard wings, mixed with bustard—the dark small spotted bustard feather is best for this river, the light coloured for Scotland and Wales—golden pheasant tail and neck, peacock wing, wood-duck feelers of blue and yellow macaw, and a black head. Hook No. 8 or 9. This is a great favourite.

No. 2. Scarlet body, scarlet hackle, and mallard wing, gold over body, topping for tail, and one in the centre of the wings, jay at the shoulder, and a black head. Hook No. 8. Large for the Spring, and B, BB for June and July.

No. 3. Fiery brown body, brown-red hackle, gold tinsel, mallard wings with a little wood-duck and golden pheasant neck feather mixed with it, macaw feelers, and a small topping for tail mixed with wood-duck. Hook BB or G. Grouse hackle round the shoulder, and a black head.

No. 4. Body yellow pig hair, half way up from the tail, the remainder wine purple or dark blue, a purple hackle over it, and a claret one at the shoulder; blue head picked out the colour of the sky; two toppings in the centre of wings of mallard and brown turkey mixed, and macaw feeler. Hook No. 9. Silver tinsel over the body.

No. 5. Orange body, broad gold tinsel, dark brown-red hackle over it; strips of wood-duck and neck feather for tail; strips of spotted Argus pheasant; a dark full mallard wing with two neck feathers in the centre, and a black head. Hook No. 9, BB, or 8. Large for high water or deep places.

No. 6. A puce body, ribbed with silver tinsel and gold twist, topping in the tail mixed with wood-duck fibres; puce hackle struck full up to the head, blue jay here, and kingfisher each side of the wings, which are of a very nice mixture of Argus pheasant small spotted feather, peacock wings, mallard, teal, guinea hen, kite tail, pheasant tail, blue and orange macaw, scarlet macaw, green parrot tails, Ibis, and silver pheasant tail (the hen); feelers of macaw, a topping over all, with the crest feather of the Hymalean pheasant, and a bronze head. Hook, Nos. 9 and 8. These, with the eleven flies in the Plates, and No. 12, early in the Spring, with the five Shannon flies, are all "first-rate killers," indeed, the fourteen painted flies are all capital ones for this river.

The Trout Flies are generally the same as those in the catalogue of flies for the season. In the spring they run rather large, but in the summer months they are used very small. Olive flies of various hues are very much used, and a fly with a green body and the feather off the root of the landrail's wing; another with orange body, black-red hackle, and woodcock wings. Hooks No. 8, in spring, Nos. 10 and 12, in summer. The various browns are capital in the early season, and the green olive, sooty olive, hare's ear and olive, brown and olive flies made full in the wings, and to be longer than the body. There are no hackles used in the spring, till a little further on in the season, then hackle flies are used; the wren tails of different sorts are very much prized, and the light red-brown grouse hackle, and yellow body; a blue body fly, black hackle, and wings of the starling; a gosling green olive fly, with mallard wings, mixed with landrail, and a hook No. 8 or 10; a fly with a yellow body of silk, red hackle dyed yellow, starling wing mixed with mallard, and a little partridge tail; the golden wren is good; a very small black gnat is good; and the never-failing "blue blow." The body of this little fly, as used on the Bann, is mole's fur mixed with golden olive, picked out at the shoulder, and a black bird's wing, to be fished with on warm sultry days. These flies are killers, and the trout are fond of them, which will be found excellent and plentiful at Portna.

On the shores of Lough Neagh, towards the Bridge of Toome, where the river issues out of the lake, there is good angling in the Drake season in June. There is a small inn at Toome Bridge, where the angler can procure a boat. It is but four miles north of "Randalstown," on the Belfast and Ballymena Railway. I have spent many a day on these waters, when a young man.

From Shane's Castle, the Earl O'Neil's, to the bridge, and from the town of Antrim to Shane's Castle, there are large trout taken with the fly; at the end of May, and throughout June, the whole surface of the lake along the shore is covered with the natural fly. The Drake, in the Plate, would be a good one made on a large size hook, to throw amongst them. Earl O'Neil grants permission to gentlemen to fly-fish in the demesne of Shane's Castle, by sending a note from the inn at Randalstown, to the Steward.

There are numerous rivers running into Lough Neagh, from five different counties, which it borders. The Bann rises in the Mourne Mountains, in the County of Down, and passing through the Lough, issues out of it at the Bridge of Toome, forming a stupendous body of fresh water. The Lough is twenty-three miles long, and twelve in width.

To get at the various small trout rivers running into all these great lakes in the north of Ireland, I would recommend, to gain information of the cross-roads, Leigh's Road Book of Ireland and Dublin Railway Guide.

The angler will now take his departure from the north and proceed to Dublin, *viâ* Belfast and Draugheda, at this place he comes to the river Boyne, where he may spend a few pleasant days at "Old Bridge," a place about three miles up the river at the "weirs." There is good Salmon fishing at this place when the tide is out, and on the flow of the tide he will take capital Grilse and Sea-Trout.

For the Boyne, the best flies are claret, brown, olive, green, orange, and black, with brown mallard wings, and turkey tail feathers. Plain ones in general are best.

LAKES OF WESTMEATH.

After leaving Draugheda, the angler will reach Dublin by rail in a very short time, where he will take his place in the railway carriage for Mullingar, the county town of Westmeath; here, he is in the centre of numerous fine lakes, well stored with large trout that will take the fly most freely in May and June; the whole country round this place is most pleasingly diversified by romantic sites, gentlemen's mansions, and extensive lakes.

There are two lakes in the neighbourhood, or environs of Mullingar, which are "Lough Ennel" and "Lough Owel," to the north of the town; the first named one is the best for large trout. There are good boats and fishermen to be had here. A little farther northward is Lough Iron, and the river Jenny, which takes its course to the Shannon. The best lake of them all is "Derevaragh," still further to the north; the town of Castlepollard is the best station to stay to fish this fine lake; the trout run twelve and fourteen pounds in it.

Lough Lane and Dromore are close to the last named lake. The angling in May is most excellent, with the green drake; it is called the drake season, and at this period the largest fish are caught; the green drake which I have described, is the right sort for the lakes, with large whole upright wings double the ordinary size.

The trout flies in general are brown, green, grey, red, black, hare's ear and yellow, hare's ear and brown, hare's ear and olive, fiery brown, claret, orange, and yellow flies, and in rough weather gaudy grilse flies are good.

The flexible minnow would be a capital bait, drawn after the boat, when the trout are not inclined to take the fly.—See an angling tour of the lakes by "Jeffery Green Drake."

There is very good salmon and trout fishing to be had in the County Tipperary, at the town of Cahir, situated on the Suir; Kilcommon Cottage on the river side, is a place of great beauty, and the angler may amuse himself in the demesne of Lord Cahir, which contains 560 acres;

this place and Clonmel may be reached by railway from Dublin, and on arriving at Kilkenny there is very good fishing in the river Barrow at the town, on the road to Cahir.

There is a small river called Killmacow, two miles above Waterford, running into the Suir, in which there is beautiful trout fishing, in the Spring and June.

There are some nice streams in Wexford, for salmon and trout fishing. The "Slaney," at Scarrawalsh Bridge, near the Barony Forth, is capital for sea trout, in August and the early Spring; there is good trout fishing the higher you proceed up this fine river.

In Lord Courtown's demesne, beyond Tara Hill, there is good grilse and sea trout fishing, the river runs through the town of Ballycannew, a few miles above Gorey; Lord Courtown's is not far from Gorey, who will allow any gentleman to angle with the fly in his charming demesne. They say that his lordship can contrive to "fish these fish" into the kettle alive out of the river, part of which runs under the mansion; I cannot tell how true this may be, the river runs close to the house, in which there are plenty of salmon and trout.

The flies used here are rather gaudy, sea trout size; and the list of flies for the season will answer admirably for trout fishing.

From the above place the angler may conveniently visit the rivers in the County Wicklow, which are all trout streams, arriving at Arklow, on the river Ovoca.

There is a very nice river[4] running along the southern side of the Wicklow Mountains, passing by a place called "Little Aghrim," from whence to the wooden bridge, three miles from Arklow, there is excellent trout fishing in March, April, and May; it passes through a long lough or piece of deep water, out of which the trout issue in the spring into the river; there is no obstruction on its banks from the Wooden Bridge Inn up to Aghrim. There is a bridge crosses the river three miles up from the

---

[4] **FOOTNOTE:** The River Derry.

Wooden Bridge, where the angler may fish up to Aghrim or down to the "Meetings." The Wooden Bridge is called the "Lower Meetings of the Waters,"—this is the most beautiful place of any in the neighbourhood of the Vale of Ovoca, as you can see fine vales from the mount behind the Inn; although from the grounds of Howard Castle, where the little and great Avon meet, the views are sublime,—this is Moore's "Sweet Vale of Ovoca, where the bright waters meet."

From the town of Rathdrum to the Meetings there is good fly fishing in the spring; through the vale there is no angling in the river, in consequence of the copper mine water running into it from the hills on each side, Cronebane, and Balymurtagh.

There is very little fishing in the river Dargle, as the stream is so small, but the scenery is magnificent, particularly in the vicinity of Powers Court Waterfall, it is about two miles and a half from the village of Powers Court.

The best way to go from Dublin to fish the rivers "Avon" and "Derry," would be through Bray and Rathdrum; begin here to fish the Avon, to the Bridge at Howard Castle; and from the Wooden Bridge angle up the Derry to Aghrim, I never saw so many small trout in my life as there are in this beautiful stream, in the spring; there are numbers of small rivers descending the Wicklow Mountains, towards the east, south, and west, in which the trout run small.

We will return to Dublin and pay a visit to the once celebrated "salmon leap," at Leixlip, a few miles west of the City—this is a charming place, where a few days may be spent to advantage; the groves and rocks, and the romantic glen are the theme of admiration. And the Park of Castletown, the most beautiful in the Kingdom; from the ancient castle at the end of the town there are views of the river and waterfall. The salmon fishing has been spoiled here by the sewers of the City running into the Liffey.

At New Bridge, on the banks of the Liffey, the station before you come to Kildare, on the Cork railroad, close to the celebrated "Curragh of Kildare," a race course of 3000 acres of verdant plain, there is capital trout fishing in April and May, and pretty fair sport may be had throughout the summer; the flies to suit the river Liffey are very small, and those little ones in my list for the season will answer well.

THE RIVER LEE, AT CORK,

Would be as good a place as any in Ireland "to go to fish," were it not for the "weirs," and foul play in many ways, which is practised all the way up, on the poor salmon; there is some little sport to be had in it in the spring, and after heavy rains. The flies to suit it are rather plain and small, blue, grey, brown, claret, and green; mallard wings, mixed with a little golden pheasant tail and neck feathers; blue macaw feelers, black head, and mixed tails like the wings. Hook B CC, in high water BB and No. 9.

SALMON RIVERS OF SCOTLAND.

We will bid adieu to old Ireland for a season, and its fair city Dublin, "with the blue sky over it," and step into the steam boat at Kingston for Holyhead, seat ourselves in a carriage, and trundle off to bonny Scotland—a country of many waters, stored with fine fish; we cross the Tweed, at Berwick, of pastoral fame, and dash into "Auld Reekey" with flying colours in no time.

The beautiful city of Edinburgh must not be left without viewing it from end to end, as it is worth while to spend a day or two in it, if you have not been there, were it only to inspect its monuments and antiquities, which are numerous, in fact, the city at large is a complete curiosity. From here the angler will be able to take rail for Perth, on the banks of the famous "river Tay;" and as the line touches on Stirling, should it be convenient, there might be a day or two spent on the Forth. There are abundance of trout about four miles up the river, and some salmon; small plain flies suit it best.

THE RIVER TAY.

This beautiful salmon river is the principal one in Perthshire, in its course it expands into Loch Tay, on leaving which it finds itself a channel and becomes rapid for miles; it has a long course, passing the towns of Dunkeld and Perth, and falls into the sea at Dundee.

The river Erne, after a long and rapid course falls into the Tay below Perth. There is also the "Timel," at the pass of Cillecrankey, on the road to Inverness from Dunkeld, and is fourteen miles from the latter place, there is a small inn close to the river, in which there is good trout fishing; the coach from Perth stops here to change horses and breakfast; it is a fine rushing stream. And also the "Keith," at Blair Dummond, where there is a very high waterfall, the sound of which can be heard at some distance; it falls into the Tay.

There is excellent angling for salmon and sea trout in the river Tay, five or six miles above Perth, in September and October; the white trout are in abundance in this river in the latter month; the salmon run very large in this water, in April, May, and June; and are best taken with large salmon flies of rather a sombre hue.

At the town of Dunkeld there is famous fishing in the Spring and Autumn. From Dundee to Perth and Dunkeld, through the "Carse of Gowrie," the Valley of the Tay is one of the most beautiful parts of all Scotland, in my estimation; at both sides of the river it is interspersed with excellent gentlemen's seats, and beautiful grounds.

There is a fishery a little above the Bridge of Perth, which is very productive.

The flies to suit this fine river are:—

No. 1. Brown pig hair bodies, ribbed with gold, dark brown-red hackle, wings light brown spotted turkey tail, red tag, and a scarlet joint above it; the body to be made long and taper. Hook No. 8. Rather large for the spring.

No. 2. A bronze peacock harl body, ribbed with gold tinsel, a brown-red hackle, and wings of mallard mixed with hen pheasant tail, the tail of the golden pheasant, red tail of mohair cut short, and the body to be thin. No. 9 hook.

No. 3. Brown mohair body, with a long red-brown spotted grouse hackle; the wings a mixture of mallard, brown turkey, and a little hen pheasant tail. Hook No. 8 or 9.

No. 4. A puce mohair body ribbed with silver, purple hackle over it, yellow tail of small topping, and a yellow hackle round the shoulder; wings of golden pheasant tail, with a little spotted bustard, a topping over all, and a black head. Hook No. 8 or 9. (A piece of wood-duck each side.)

No. 5. An orange body ribbed with black silk and gold tinsel, topping in the tail, and a black-red hackle over it, (a hackle with the black streak running all the way through it); scarlet tag and tail; wings light brown turkey tail, rather lighter at the tips, a few fibres of wood-duck each side, the same quantity of bustard, and a bronze head. Hook No. 9, or for high water, No. 7.

This fly will be found an excellent killer in the Tay, or any other river in Scotland.

These, with the twelve painted and engraved flies, no man can desire better. Nos. 3, 4, 5, and 11, will be found excellent in low water, and Nos. 6, 7, 8, 9, and 10, in high water.

The Sea-Trout Flies are orange bodies, mixed wings, jay at shoulder, silver tinsel, and a small topping for tail. Hook *fff* or C, say No. 6, Kendal.

Blue body, black hackle ribbed with silver, and mallard wings. Hook CC.

Green body, black hackle, gold twist, and dark brown turkey wings.

Light brown body, red hackle, gold twist, two fibres of red Ibis for tail, and glede wings. Hook No. 6 or 7. In low water they take them rather small, with the tinsel, of course.

Hare's ear body, ribbed with silver twist, a greyish dark hackle, the colour of the dark fur on the ear, mallard wings, and tail of the same. Make another fly mixed with orange and yellow mohair.

A black fly ribbed with silver tinsel, black wing with white tips, black hackle, and a yellow head and tail. Hook C.

It would be as well to try very small gaudy flies occasionally, as you may rise a grilse during the time you are fishing for white-trout. A grilse loves to rise at a middling gaudy fly after leaving the sea. Blue, green, and red flies are all good.

I will give three more favorites that will not miss:—

No. 1. Body brown claret colour, mixed with the fur of hare's ear, ribbed with silver twist, a short black hackle, wings rather light brown mallard, and a black head. Hook, Green Drake size, or No. 6.

No. 2. A black body, tipped with orange silk, ribbed with silver twist, a black hackle, and dark brown turkey tail wings. Hook No. 6 or C, varied with blue body and black-red hackle.

No. 3. A blue dun body, a dun hackle ribbed with silver twist, tail two fibres of mallard, and grey mallard for wings. Hook C, or No. 6. A fly with an olive body, and one with yellow and mallard wings, are good. These flies will be found great killers where the fish are plentiful, with a good ripple on the water, and would do admirably on the Dee and Don, at Aberdeen.

THE DEE AND DON.

These rivers run into the sea at Aberdeen, and are excellent for Salmon and Trout fishing—the Dee for Salmon, and the Don more for Trout, which are most delicious for the table; they cut as pink as Salmon. The white-trout fishing is good here in October, and the flies I have just given for the Tay will kill admirably in these rivers; and for salmon, will be capital ones, made a size or two larger. When I visited that country a few years back, I walked up the Dee one evening, and at a shallow ford, above the bridge, there were two men "stroke-hauling" the salmon as they run up out of the pool below, and which they called their rented fishery; they rushed into the stream with a sort of net in their hands, and had them out in quick time. As the fish run, the water did not appear to cover their backs. I was told, were it not for this practice, the river would be swarming.

THE RIVER SPEY.

This splendid Salmon river runs through Elginshire, and a nobler one there is not to be found for fishing with the salmon fly, particularly in high water, and in the large pools when the water is low. In summer there is little sport to be had, except in these pools, with a good ripple, and towards the sea, from the bridge at Fochabers, a capital station, with an excellent inn. Early in the morning and late in the evening, are the best times in the heat of summer. I had a fly sent me some years past, by McPherson Grant, about the size of C or drake size, with which he killed a salmon, twenty pounds weight, in the Spey. The body of the fly was made of yellow silk, red cock's hackle, toucan tail ribbed with gold, jay at the shoulder, a neat gaudily mixed wing, feelers of blue and yellow macaw, and a small black head. It was one of my flies, which, if made on large size hooks, will kill anywhere. The above little fly is just the sort for low water, and should be adopted, made very small, in the summer months. The salmon should be thrown for with this sort of fly, in rapid currents rushing into deep holes, where the fish lie. The winged larva would do well in such places for grilse and sea-trout. In the spring, flies the size of No. 12, are used, with long thin silk bodies of orange, yellow, red, and green colours, red hackles, jay and mixed wings, with red feathers prevailing in them, and black heads, ribbed with gold and silver tinsel. The fifteen painted Salmon Flies will be found great killers in this river, varied in size according to the state of the water.

There is a river which runs past the town of Banff, the Keith, in which there is good angling a few miles up from the broad part of the water. Guinea hen and jay hackles kill here, with grouse and brown body, mallard wings mixed with turkey tail, and small size hooks, say CC or B.

THE FINDHORN

is another fine Salmon river after heavy rains, which swell it to a prodigious size, as shown by its channel in low water, high ridges of sand and gravel being thrown up on each side of its banks at every flat running ford in its course to the sea. The flies to suit it are:—

No. 1. Brown body, gold tinsel, wings copper-coloured mallard, and a brown grouse hackle. Hook No. 8, and BB.

No. 2. Body brown floss silk, ribbed with silver, large motley brown cock's tail feather over the body, and a spotted turkey tail for wings. No. 9 hook.

No. 3. Body, puce floss silk ribbed with silver, black-red hackle, a mixed wing of glede, turkey tail, and mallard, with a topping over all, and a dark claret or purple hackle. Hook No. 9.

No. 4. Light puce body with a hackle of the same colour, topping for tail, and a gaudily mixed wing, (not too much so) broad silver. No. 8 hook.

No. 5. Yellow body, puce hackle, mixed wings, rib of silver, and tail a topping. Hook No. 9. These, with the painted ones, will do the work to a nicety in this dashing river.

The River Nairne, in these quarters, is not a bad one for grilse and salmon fishing in September; the town of Nairne, is the most convenient station, beginning a few miles up, and proceeding higher; the small salmon flies that I have given for the Spey will suit this river well.

RIVERS AND LAKES ADJACENT TO FORT WILLIAM, ON THE CALEDONIAN CANAL.

These wild and majestic scenes in the heart of the Highlands of Scotland are without doubt splendid, either to look upon or for the purpose of salmon and trout fishing, the recollections of such to the intelli-intelligent and contemplative mind of the gentle angler who has visited this region, must be lasting and agreeable.[5] The sail down the Clyde from Glasgow, passing Dumbarton Castle (on a rock in the water to the right), to Greenock, is most enchanting; opposite this fine town the angler will observe a grand expanse of deep and blue salt water, bordered in the distance with mountains dark and high, filling the imagination with awe, while pacing the decks of the frail but well appointed little steam boat Helen McGregor in the gloom, as she creaks away through briny silvered waves of lakes, estuaries, and straits, to Caledonia's "noblest work"—the Great Canal. Rounding a rough northern head land, where seven currents meet, of seas, sounds, and straits, Crenan in the wake, compassing the shore in Jura Sound, the "little Helen" struggling with the swelling tide, appeared to be standing still though at full speed; Loch Etive, on the starboard—into whose bosom, Awe's serpentine waters steal at solitary "Bunaw;" Lismore in the distance, Mull in our wake, due West—the rapid subsiding—through it "the fair one" tripped gallantly. In these "meetings of the waters," what oceans of salmon sported and played at large in their blue and fresh element, far from the wily bars! The "Heroine" seemed at once to be stepping up hills from lock to lock, till she levelled the base of "Ben Nevis;" close to which mighty mountain, the "fair one" squatted for the night. Glad enough were her living freight to get on firm footing, and wend their way across a mossy plain, without a rolling stone, to a little house under a hill, that kept beds "well aired," and "usquebaugh," for travellers. At the dawn of morning, through the haze,

---

[5] **FOOTNOTE:** The Author's trip.

could be descried, "Fair Helen," smoking—her steam was up—sitting, "sidey for sidey," by the lofty Ben, the sight of which, to look up at, was staggering. He had yet his nightcap on of hazy grey, but enough of the giant hill could be denoted that his base on that side was hewn away, facilitating the great track. This morning, away went the "fair one," rattling like "sticks a breaking." Hurrah for Fort William—a voice, "and the Camerons of Lochiel,"—here we are at Crystal Laggan, Lochiel, and Lochey's excellent waters for the Salmon Trout—(I will give the flies to suit them a little further on). "Fair Helen" began her movements slowly for some time, creeping through locks, o'er hills, in basins—Macomer on the starboard,—Lochiel, farewell!—now skimming into saltless "Lochey's" (famed for its ancient mountain clans) soft and balmy waters; through the lake she dashed, breast high—a strait ahead—steaming by Balalister at seven knots by the log, soundings the deep nine, "Fair Helen" entered the gorge, and now rushing down an inclined plain, to the fear of the timid, and delight of the stouthearted, double quick did run the "fair one," making up for lost time experienced in the "meeting of the waters"—through lock gates, up hills, &c., now through an embankment, nearing Fort Augustus, and the head of Lochness, down she settled between two stupendous lock gates. "What aw-fu' gates!" What work bestowed on them—what an enormous depth are they—the wet and muddy sides of which beat chilly. Down, "down below," went the "fair one," till she levelled the golden waters of—"O, that lovely lake,"—into which she slipped like a fairy elf. After her cold incarceration, "Helen the Fair" tripped merrily down the centre of the "fathomless Lochness," the sun breaking, beamed out upon us cheeringly after the chill and hazy morning. Like looking-glass did that sun-lit lake appear, stretching away before us, losing itself in the distance, bordered by hills and mountains on either side, till on the larboard was seen Morrison's lonely glen and meandering stream. We neared the bay, sounded whistle, and lowered steam. A few minutes more, and off went the Helen McGregor, making head like a waddling duck through the valley of golden[6] waters. Hush! The mountain sylph is heard in the cabin. Hush! by the powers, it's Phillips, warbling the incantation of the wizard of the glen.

---

[6] **FOOTNOTE:** There is a kind of slimy weed, of a yellow colour, that is produced at the bottom of the lake, which causes that appearance, and is injurious to fly fishing in the river.

"Farewell to the mountain,
And sun-lighted vale."

O, shade of Wilson! the soul of Scottish song. Angler, may you rest in peace. On the starboard was observed the "Falls of Fyres," descending, perpendicularly, over a craggy precipice—most curious. "Bonny Helen" slid smoothly along, till, at the "heel of the evening," we entered the last embankment of Caledonia's Grand Canal, just where the beautiful river Ness issues out of "that lake," opening into a lovely and fertile valley, in the centre of which is a boat upset, an antiquity, covered with motley trees. A few minutes more and we were safely landed at the quay of the fair and sweet metropolis of the ancient Highlands, Inverness, seated on a hill above the river. O, I sigh for the days that will never return! High and airy rock, I split upon you twice, steering northwise fra' bonny Dundee, through the "Carse o' Gowrie," by Laburnam, to famed Dunkeld, on Tay's noble waters; Blair Athol and Fore's Macbeth crossed the source of Spay, through a waste and dreary plain, with villages far apart, where ran those weirdy thinly kilted lads to see the "four-in-hand;" up hill, down dale, and heathered moor we steered, till at length we galloped towards the glooming, by the graves of dark Culloden's bloodstained field—nearing the city, on went the drag, and over a well macadamised road, "knapped" by the hardy highland wight, we hurried into Inverness. Alas! this bronchial asthma, that shuts me from that fishing. Fond memory brings the light of other days around me.

SALMON FLIES FOR FORT WILLIAM, &c.

The flies to suit the various waters surrounding Fort William are generally of a medium size and middling gaudy. The engraved ones in my list, for Salmon in general, from No. 2 to 11, will kill well. The list for the season for Trout.

No. 1. Light blue body, rib of silver, guinea hen hackle, blue jay, topping in tail; wings, teal, mallard, guinea hen rump feather, peacock wing feather, and blue and yellow feelers of macaw. No. 9 hook, or BB.

No. 2. A small size fly like the above, varied with black floss body. A good sort for the Lochy. Hook C or CC.

No. 3. A fly like the first, varied in the body thus: yellow tag, silver tints, and a small topping for tail; a blue mohair joint, then a red one, another blue joint, then an orange one under the fly at the shoulder, and a blue head. Hook No. 9 or BB; a C for lake Trout.

No. 4. A claret fly, with wings and tail like the first one, varied with yellow-brown body and hackle, and ribbed with gold. BB hook, and CC for lake Trout, with a bronze head.

No. 5. A fly with grass-green floss silk, ribbed with gold, black-red hackle, and blue head; the wings and tail like the first. Vary the body with different greens. Hooks from CC up to No. 9.

No. 6. A black body, with black legs, silver tinsel and cock of the north rump feathers for the wings; some call it the "copperkeilsey." Hook C, CC and B. This is the celebrated Kenloch of Kenloch.

SALMON FLIES FOR THE NESS.

No. 1. Body half black and yellow, a jay and purple hackle ribbed with silver, orange head, mallard, peacock wing and jungle cock wings. Hook BB.

No. 2. Body black hair, orange tag, ribbed with gold and silver, black hackle, jay at the shoulder, wings mixed, of guinea hen, teal, two small tipped feathers, and two toppings over all a little longer, tail a small topping, and a bronze head. Hook B or BB. This will be found a great killer in the Ness and Beauley, a beautiful stream at the head of the Murray Firth.

No. 3. Body yellow-brown pig hair, ribbed with gold, small, topping for tail, red cock's hackle and blue jay, wings of golden pheasant tail, mixed with mallard, neck feather, teal, and guinea hen, green parrot and macaw feelers, and a black head. Hook No. 9 or B; for low water, C. This is a capital fly for either the Ness or Beauley. These, with the painted flies, made small, will suit well.

There is a kind of yellowish slimy weed on the bottom of the Ness which proceeds from Loch Ness, that is injurious to the propagation of the salmon of late years, and it affects the fly fishing considerably, to the great disappointment and vexation of the good anglers of the north.

THE RIVER SHIN.

Classic Shin, on whose heath-clad banks and flowing waters the great and good fly fishers roam, who never saw "Kelt of Baggit" there—the haunt of monarchs of the sea, and shepherd swains that watch His flocks, and feed His Dams—the theme of poetess, and the learned. O, "Ephemera," how beautifully written is that "Book of the Salmon;" how exquisitely delineated that "Ova;" how admirably that "golden fish," which bounds up falls and cataracts in that purling "meandering" stream; how charming to gaze upon that lovely "Goddess of the Brooks"—the famed Ondine—how rightly represented. Oh! excellent "Ephemera"—my good and constant friend—the "great and good Will Blacker's" tears (I blush) descend like rain through these sky lights, and damp the very sheets my palsied pen doth blot. Alas! well-a-day-that noble salmon fishing—what sport! These lean and bellows'd sides are winded—this flattened chest, once full, now dented—these calves, once plump, now thin and gone—these shins, once clad, are now protruding. The "puss" more chronic heaves, yes, I still can fish! These cheeks, how pale (their bones "can't grind"), once rosy, the pride of more than "Reva's" lovely blooming rose, my blessed bosom friend, my wife, whose lamp is trimmed. O, "Ephemera!" friend, when shall we meet, with rod in hand, on pure and crystal Shin?—

"When summer comes,
The heather bells entice,
Our feet to roam.
The mournful dove,
Within the dale invites,
To peace and love."

O, summer's glorious sun! I await thee, to tan this shrivelled, shorn hide. O! come, and regenerate this sapless tree with heavenly warmth.

> My heart's in the Highlands,
> My heart is not here;
> My heart's in the Highlands,
> Chasing the deer,
> Chasing the wild deer,
> And following the roe,
> My heart's in the Highlands,
> Wherever I go.

I cannot add a fly to the list for the Shin in the "Book of the Salmon," by "Ephemera," except that I submit to the notice of the great salmon fishers of Shin those model flies in my list for trial, which, no doubt, will kill. I never fished the Shin, although I have been twice near it. Mr. Young, of Invershin, the renter of the river, will show gentlemen angling there every possible facility, civility, and politeness. The "Queen's Gap," in the cruives, is lifted on sabbath days.

THE RIVER THURSO.

The Thurso, famed for its fresh run salmon throughout the year, is the most northern river in Scotland. The town of Thurso, in Caithness-shire, is the best station, and the route, from Aberdeen to Wick.

The salmon flies for Thurso are rather of a plain and sombre cast, varying in size through the fishing months. The river is remarkably high and full in the spring, in consequence of the melting of the snow and ice, and at that period requires large flies, like No. 12; further on in the season they are much smaller in size, like Nos. 1, 2, 3, to No. 11, which are capital ones for it, and the other engravings are likewise good in low water for the fresh run grilse. Throughout the summer months the following are also good for this river:—

No. 1. Body black floss silk, orange tag, tip of gold, small topping for tail, black-red hackle, mallard wings mixed with peacock wing, a topping over all, and a black head. Hook BB, B.

No. 2. Body claret silk, claret hackle, ribbed with gold, a short topping tail, with silver tip, mallard wings mixed with tipped feathers, macaw feelers, and a black head. Hook No. 9, or B. This is an admirable fly for lake trout, on C hook.

No. 3. Body yellow-brown mohair, red hackle, a short topping for tail, ribbed with gold, claret hackle round the shoulder, and mixed wings rather grey, and inclined to be gaudy. No. 9 hook, or BB. C, for lake trout.

No. 4. A black fly, with yellow head, tail of mohair, black hackle, ribbed with broad silver, wings black turkey tail with white tip, varied with brown turkey tail. A fly of each is useful. Hook No. 8 or 9.

No. 5. A green fly, both body and hackle, mixed wings rather gaudy, ribbed with gold, orange head, topping in tail, varied with a black-red hackle, and light green silk body ribbed with gold twist. Hook B or BB.

No. 6. A dark brown fly, brown red hackle and body, ribbed with gold twist, and glede wings, varied with brown spotted turkey tail feather or mallard, one of each. Hook No. 8 or 9, B for low water.

There is a good deal of guinea hen and teal feathers used in the flies of these northern rivers, which appears to be an improvement, with jungle-cock and wood-duck.

There is a river issues out of Loch Naver, a short way from the source of the Thurso, which falls into the sea in the same direction west of the town of Thurso; it has a winding course, and would be a very good river for salmon were it well preserved.

There are numerous rivers running into the firths on the east side of Sutherland, which produce salmon and fine trout that run up from the sea:—the Wick and Helmsdale in Caithness, the Brora near Golspie, the Dornoch into which the river Shin flows, Drummond and Loch Clash, Dingwall river and lake, and the river Beauley at the head of the Murray Firth.

Lord Lovat is the owner of this river, and he is very willing to grant permission to gentlemen to fish on sending in their cards.

THE RIVER ESK.

The North and South Esk are rivers of Forfar, falling into the sea near Montrose. The North Esk is the best of the two, and affords excellent angling for salmon and sea-trout in August and September. These rivers may be visited by rail from Aberdeen or Dundee, at the present day. I have been told by a gentleman residing at Forfar, that the North Esk was sometimes swarming with salmon and grilse to an incredible extent. The wealthy proprietor of the river will give instant permission to gentlemen to fly fish, information of which he can obtain at the town of Montrose, on the Great Northern Railroad.

The flies to suit these rivers are small and plain. A small claret fly with mallard wings; a fly with brown body and a furnace hackle, mallard wings mixed with blue peacock neck feather, strips of mallard in tail, and gold. Hook C or CC.

An orange body fly of floss silk, a black hackle, gold, the wings mixed of light and dark mallard, the light feathers are found under the wings of the wild drake on the body, the brown copper-coloured ones on its back growing down from the roots of the wings, (use floss silk for the bodies). A black fly, with silver and black hackle, and teal wings mixed with blue peacock neck. Hook C or CC.

LOCH LEVEN.

The trout fly fisher staying at Stirling, or its neighbourhood, on the Great Northern, will find himself agreeably situated in the centre of many beautiful streams, to which he may have easy access. At the town of Kinross, by the head of Loch Leven, is a nice station for the lake, and at the village of Largo, to fish the river Leven, below which place it enters the sea at the mouth of the Firth of Forth. A short distance from Largo, near the Promontory, is the town of Anstruther, famous for a monument to the memory of "Maggy Lauder." I had the pleasure of once seeing it.

On the Edinburgh and Northern line from Stirling, is the town of Kettle, on the "River Eden," a good station. There are grilse and sea-trout run up it out of the bay of St. Andrew's, in the spring and autumn. Try about the town of Cupar, and near its source, at "Auchtermuchty."

The flies to suit it are, hare's ears, black hackles, red hackles, and furnace flies, varied in size.

THE RIVER ALLAN.

This is a good stream for trout fishing; it enters the Forth below Stirling, just above the town of Aloa. It has an extraordinary winding course, flowing through a picturesque country, and famed in poetic lore as "Allan's winding stream."

> "On the banks of Allan water,
> When the sweet spring time did fall,
> Lived the miller's lovely daughter,
> The fairest of them all.
> For his bride a soldier sought her,
> And a winning tongue had he;
> On the banks of Allan's water,
> There was none so gay as she."

Sea-trout and grilse run up the Allan in spring and autumn, which afford good sport. The small trout flies in my list suit this river capitally.

A few miles above Stirling there is good fishing up to Loch Katrine, commencing below the town of Dumblane, on the Scottish Central Line, and fish up to "Callander," on the east of Ben Lomond. Dumblane is famed as the birth place of "Charming Jessie," in Burns' poetic muse—

> "The sun had gan' doun
> O'er the lofty Ben Lomond,
> And left the red clouds
> To preside o'er the scene,
> When lanely I stray'd in
> The calm summer gla'ming,

William Blacker

To muse on sweet Jessie,
The flower of Dumblane."

There is another stream that runs down from "Aberfildy" to Stirling, in which there is excellent trout fishing. It has a winding course, falling over rocks, rushing through gorges, down precipices in its way, where it forms deep holes for itself, which in the summer are the haunts of large and fine trout.

The flies to suit it are, small dark hare's ears, small black hackles, red and black ants, browns, small duns, and hare's ear and yellow, the blue blow, the brown midge, and in the spring, the March brown, and stone fly, for large fish.

There is a very nice stream running out of "Loch Lomond" into the river Clyde, at the town of Dumbarton, in which there are sea-trout in the spring and autumn. They take very small dun flies, silver greys and black midges, the dark hare's ear, and red hackle.

The picturesque Loch Lomond affords good trout fishing along its gravelly shores, and near the islands. There are two flies that kill well in it, which are as follows: Black body and hackle, tip of silver, wings of the short bronze feathers of the back of the peacock. No. 6 hook, or *fff*. The other one is, red body, red hackle, and a wing like the first, both tailed with two fibres of the feather of the wings. I received these two flies from a gentleman, one time when I was at Glasgow, who confirmed them as "out-and-outers."

There are fish called Pullen, very numerous in Loch Lomond, the shape and size of herrings, which are also numerous in Loch Neagh, in the north of Ireland. They sell in Belfast as "fresh water herrings."

When a young man, I denominated Belfast my favorite home, among my dear friends of the rod and gun. Newry, in the County of Down, was the home of my ancestors. My first crying was behind "Cronebaun" hills, in the County of Wicklow, near the "Ovoca," famed for "sweetness" and poetic muse of Erin's humble bard, Tom Moore.

Looking over the Wicklow sands, where many a poor fisherman foundered, in the village[7] of "Red Cross," was the first sight my "mama" got of me; like a cloistered nun, I was covered in a veil, which, they say, would always keep me from the "briny depths." Many "crosses" have I had since January 14th, 1814, the "hard winter" which corresponds with that of last year. Mature years of experience make wise men. Forty and one summers having rolled over my head, the dishevelled ringlets of which are now sprinkled with "honorable grey"—bashful man, hide your blushes—my ruddy tint flies when I tell you, my dear anglers, that my sincere desire is to love every good man, as God has taught me. There is no one I despise, disposed at all times to revere superiors, condescend to those who perchance may be my inferiors, continent to kind friends, and forgiving to enemies, if any. Unless we profit by charity, all other profit seems void.

LOCH AWE AND RIVER.

This celebrated lake, on the western side of Scotland, may be conveniently reached from Glasgow. There are steam boats sail two or three times a week up Loch Fine to Inverary, where there can be every information gained respecting conveyances to the inn at Loch Awe, where boats and men are to be had. It is a long and narrow lake in places, and in summer most cheering and pleasant to the fly fishers resorting there. Good angling may be found in the river running by Glenorchy into the lake, where it again issues out of it, and is called the River Awe.

It runs with a full and rapid stream, has but a short course, falling into the salt water lake, or estuary, called "Etive," opposite the island of Mull.

There could be no better river or lake in the kingdom for salmon, were it not for the "cruives," that, of course, "weed them all away," the proprietor of which is most obliging to grant permission to gentlemen anglers who visit it. The purity of these waters facilitates the propagation

---

[7] **FOOTNOTE:** The mansion is roofless, says "Rory O'More."

of the salmon wonderfully, were they allowed ingress and egress. When the fishing laws are altered, and a reformation made, there will be grand fly fishing, as good as can be found in Norway. In the neighbourhood of good salmon and trout fishing rivers, the people, whom the anglers employ, are very much benefited, and particularly innkeepers, on their banks, and in towns where there is not much traffic. The angler's heart is "in fishing" wherever he goes.

The salmon and trout flies to suit Loch Awe and river (my memoranda are generally correct).

No. 1. An original and most killing fly for salmon:—Body black ostrich harl, ribbed with gold, a tag of yellow mohair at the tail, tail a very short topping, a rich black-red hackle rolled over the black sparingly, and a mallard wing, made to stand well up and apart. Hook BB, or No. 9. C for lake trout.

No. 2. A brown body, black hackle ribbed with gold, and grouse wings. Hook CC.

No. 3. Bronze peacock body, ribbed with gold twist, black-red cock's hackle, and dark brown grouse rump feather mixed with turkey tail for wings. Hook BB. C for trout in the lake.

No. 4. A cinnamon fly, with glede wings mixed with jungle cock, and ribbed with gold. B hook. No. 9 for the river.

No. 5. A black body, silver tinsel, black hackle, full teal wings, yellow head, and tail. Hook B.

No. 6. A dark green fly ribbed with gold, silver pheasant tail mixed with mallard for wings, a small topping in tail, and orange head. Hook BB, or C.

A blue fly with teal wings and blue hackle ribbed with silver, topping in the tail, and red head of mohair, hook B, or BB; and a fly with peacock harl body, black hackle, hen pheasant tail wings mixed, and the tail of the cock bird. Hook B, or C for trout.

The large trout flies in my list for the season are excellent ones for the lake, and Nos. 3, 4, 5, and 11, for salmon.

There is good salmon fishing to be had in Islay, south of Mull. The steam boat from Glasgow calls there twice a week. Mr. Campbell, the laird, resides in the island, who gives permission, unhesitatingly, to gentlemen making application to him.

The river is at the landing place of the steamer; the salmon, which are numerous in it, take small gaudy flies—blue body and hackle, brown, claret, red, black, and green flies.

There is also salmon fishing to be had in "Jura Isle," a little to the north of Islay.

THE RIVERS IRVINE, GIRVAN, AND STINCHER, IN AYRSHIRE.

In this westerly quarter may be found excellent Salmon and Trout fishing in the spring and autumn in these beautiful streams, which can be reached from the city of Glasgow every day by rail.

The Stincher is the best for salmon, the flies for which are browns, blacks, reds, and greys, all plainly dressed ones. I will describe one here, a great favourite of a gentleman friend of mine, Mr. Murdoch,—Stephen Blair, &c. At Glasgow, some years ago, on my stay in that city; I give his name, as he used to call my flies "mest noble flees," and laughed heartily to see the manœuvring of the hook in my fingers.

The body of Mr. Murdoch's fly was in joints of pig hair picked out, and at the head a black-red hackle; first, there was a tip of gold, a tag of yellow hair, then a joint of orange, a joint of fiery brown, a joint of claret, and a joint of black pig hair or mohair, spaniel hair is best; the wings a light brown turkey tail feather with white tips, tied on topping a little longer than the bend of the hook, a very small topping in the tail. Hook No. 8 for high water.

Mr. Murdoch was a native of Ayr, and a keen fisher, and used to speak much of his angling in the "waters o' Doon."

From Ayr, the angler may proceed to the lakes of Cumberland, *viâ* Carlisle, Keswick, and Bowness.

RIVERS OF WALES.—THE CONWAY.

There would be excellent salmon fishing in Wales were the rivers properly preserved. The Conway (North Wales) is a beautiful stream, and it is a great pity it should be neglected; however, I believe it will be very soon protected from the nets, &c., as there are a few spirited gentlemen in the neighbourhood of Llanwrist and Aberconway, who will rent and preserve it for fly fishing only, all the way up from the town of Conway to Capel Curig. The salmon flies in my list, made on small size hooks, will suit it well, varied according to the state of the water; and my list of trout flies will be found admirable for it. Information respecting season tickets, and rules of the fishing, may be obtained at the Inn at Llanwrist.

THE RIVER DOVEY.

The Dovey is a nice stream, but runs off very soon, like all others descending from the mountains. The salmon would be, nevertheless, very plentiful in it, as there are many capital large pools for them to haunt, if they were allowed to reach them. It is so very much netted at its mouth that it cannot be possible for fly fishing to be good. The neighbourhood of Machynlleth is the best place to fly fish it. In the spring and autumn the salmon flies in the plates will be found admirable for it, made on CC hooks, and C for low water. The furnace and black-red hackles are excellent local flies, made on C hooks, for summer. Sewen take small duns, and the Cochybonddu.

RIVER TIVEY.

The Tivey is considered the very best and most prolific river in all Wales. It has a long and winding course to Cardigan, and before it reaches this place, at Newcastle Emlyn, it is a picture of a river for salmon fishing. Lampeter, higher up, is a very good station, near to which place are the "Tivey Pools," where the fish lie in low water. My list of both salmon and trout flies would be excellent for the Tivey, dressed on small hooks.

THE WYE, MONMOUTH.

The Wye, at the town of Monmouth, and up towards Leominster, is an excellent river for salmon; and the Usk, in the same quarter, is also good for salmon and fine trout. The latter river is a very short way from the Wye, and may be conveniently reached from Monmouth to Abergavenny, close to which town it passes, and enters the mouth of the Severn at Newport; the Wye falls into it higher up, at Chepstow. The painted flies in the plates will be just the sort for the Wye made smaller, and will suit the Usk admirably, dressed smaller still.

There is a local fly or two which I will give, viz.—Body yellow mohair bordering on orange, a red ginger cock's hackle long in the fibre rolled over it, ribbed with plate gold, a red tail, and light brown turkey tail feather with white tips for the wings. Hook No. 9.

Another fly with the same body, and wings of the bittern's neck, two feathers should be tied in, and the whole to stand well up.

Another fly, with brown body, brown hackle, brown wings, and tail, ribbed with gold. The Dun Palmer, in the Plate No. 7, and the Dun Salmon fly, No. 6, made on smaller size hooks, will be found excellent ones. Nos. 4, 5, and 10, are also good, the latter for high water. Never were there better flies seen for the Welsh rivers in general than these, made to suit the state of the water.

THE RIVER SEVERN.

The river Severn has its source in Montgomeryshire, takes a long course, passing the towns of Welshpool and Shrewsbury. It is a fine stream, and there could be no better one were it well preserved. There is excellent greyling fishing below Shrewsbury, but little or no salmon fishing. "Mr. Taylor," in his Book on Angling, who was a native of this place, says, "that he hooked and killed a greyling in the Severn, below Shrewsbury, five pounds weight."

The River Thame rises in Wales, near Bishop's Castle, and joins the Severn below Worcester. It produces excellent fish, particularly trout and greyling. Begin to fish at Ludlow, and move down the stream. The flies in my list are good for it.

THE TRENT

is a good river for greyling fishing, near the town of Newark, on the Nottingham and Lincoln Railroad. The flies to suit it are small blue duns, cochybonddus, small black hackles, orange duns, red hackles without wings, wren hackles, small grouse hackles, ash duns, willow flies, blue blows, &c.

The well known Lakes and Rivers of Cumberland are excellent for fly fishing, particularly Ulswater for trout, and the beautiful Lake Windermere for a fish called Char. These delicious fish take a fly like the sea-trout, which they resemble in shape, although much darker in colour. A small fly made on No. 8 hook, or No. 6, with puce body and hackle, ribbed with silver, the wings of brown mallard, and a tail the same feather as the wings; a fly with an orange body, black hackle, and mallard wings; another with woodcock wings, orange body, and furnace red hackle; a fly with a bronze peacock harl body, rib of gold, black hackle, and jay wings, varied with light grey mallard for wings; and my list of trout flies for the season will be found excellent for the trout in the lakes and rivers.

Bowness, Patterdale, Poolybridge, and Keswick, are all nice stations, where men and boats may be had conveniently.

RIVERS OF YORK AND DERBY.

The beautiful streams of these counties are excellent for trout fishing, and the scenery varied and pleasing throughout. The river Wharf is a delightful stream in the neighbourhood of Bolton Abbey, a well known place of "Hofland." See his painting of it, which gives a good idea of the magnificent scene. Harrowgate, and Harewood Bridge, would be very convenient stations for the fly fisher to stay at. The greyling are good here, and the small duns, wren, and grouse hackles, do well; the Dottrille hackle, and black and red hackle, with yellow waxed silk bodies, and starling wing, are good; a small fly with peacock body, black hackle, and starling wing. No. 13 hook, or 12. These flies may be seen in my list. They will also kill well at Driffield.

THE HODDER.

Whitewell is a favourite spot for anglers to meet during the May fly season, it is beautifully situated for scenery and sport; my list of flies will be found excellent killers in this stream for both trout and greyling; there is a comfortable inn here.

RIVERS OF DERBY.

Derbyshire is watered by many delightful streams, which abound with trout and greyling, the owners of which allow the angler to fish without the least hesitation on making application and sending in his card.

The River Dove, at "Dove Dale," is as charming a place for a few days fly fishing as any in the County, and is famed for the pleasing recollections of the early days of "Walton and Cotton's" rambles on its banks.

There is an inn at the entrance of the Dale, and Mapleton and Ashbourne convenient stations. The flies to suit the Dove are, small duns of various sorts, greys, and browns, as described in my list for the season, there cannot be better flies for it if made to answer the state of the water.

The beautiful river Wye, at the town of "Bakewell," is a capital stream for the fly, and many a good angler makes his appearance here in the drake season; the winged larva and May fly in the engraving would do well on windy days, when the natural May fly did not show itself in great numbers; my list for the season will be found excellent ones for the Wye.

The Derwent is also another nice fly-fishing stream for trout and fine greyling; the best places to proceed to fish would be Baslow and Rowsley Bridge, my list of flies will suit it well.

THE RIVERS WANDLE AND COLN.

These rivers are convenient to London, and are famous for fly fishing: they are in general private property, but the owners are very civil in granting one or two days' angling on application and sending your card. There are two or three places on the Wandle that may be angled in at will, about the neighbourhood of Carshalton, and Ackbridge; and on the Coln, at Watford and Rickmansworth. The flies to suit the Wandle are generally well known, which are—the Carshalton cocktail, dark hare's ear, blue and pale duns, little peacock fly, furnace fly, small soldier fly, and little black red palmers, the little brown midge and the March brown made very small, small black gnat, and red ant, these flies may be seen in my list for the season, they cannot fail to afford diversion.

The flies to suit the river Coln, are—the brown Caperer, large cinnamon fly, brown-red palmer, and Orl fly with a dun hackle and yellow body, the stone fly, March brown, brown grouse hackle, wren-tail fly, large red ant, black gnat, and dun drake, a red hackle fly made full with the red and grey tail feather of the partridge mixed, bronze peacock harl body. Hook No. 8.

The Great Whirling Dun, Red Spinner, the Coachman, and the Large Governor flies will be found with those good for the evening, with a nice ripple on the water.

The river Itchen, at Itchen Abbas, Hants, is a very nice stream for fly fishing, and the Avon at Salisbury Plain, the Kennet, at Hungerford, Berks, is also good, and the river Mole at Leatherhead, Surrey, is a beautiful stream for fly fishing, in the vicinity of Randal's Park. It has been preserved in the park for years, and abounds with large trout.

Whitchurch and Stockbridge are also good places for the fly, in Hampshire; and the famed "Lea" at Ware, the resort of many a good London angler; the river Stour is another fine trout stream, it receives the rivers of Wilts in its course, waters Hampshire, and falls into the sea at Christchurch. My list of flies will kill here.

There are many very beautiful rivers in Devonshire for trout fishing, which are, the Ex at Exeter and Tiverton, the Ax at Axminster, and the Tamar which separates Cornwall and Devon, a very considerable river, in which there are salmon and fine white trout in the spring of the year, March and April. Launceston would be the most convenient station for the tourist angler to fish this fine river.

The salmon in it take small flies, with claret and dark brown bodies, ribbed with gold, mallard wings mixed with a little tipped feather, and tails of the same; at high water they rise and take more gaudily dressed ones, made on B and BB hooks.

I sent the colours to a gentleman to suit this river some time ago, who told me it would be an excellent one for salmon, were it well taken care of. He made his own flies.

I have also sent fishing colours, hackles, and flies, to suit every river, or nearly so, in Great Britain, to gentlemen residing on their banks, which has been a great advantage to me in obtaining the knowledge of the local flies, but in general my flies have succeeded best in the hands of those Fly fishers who have made it their study and practice.

It will be seen that I have not withheld the local flies for each river from accompanying my own, and those great anglers who visit Norway will find the Salmon flies in the plates most killing, and it will be a great advantage to them to have this book in their possession, to give them a knowledge of fishing colours, and the various modes of dressing both salmon and trout flies, the delineation of which they will see I have given to a nicety, having studied from my youth, and learned from my own observation.

I have been all my life too fond of fishing, which has been sometimes to my disadvantage, but I loved the scenes of woods, green hills, of singing birds, meadows, and fresh air, rushing rivers, and above all, to look at the beautiful fish jumping to catch the fly on the surface of the water.

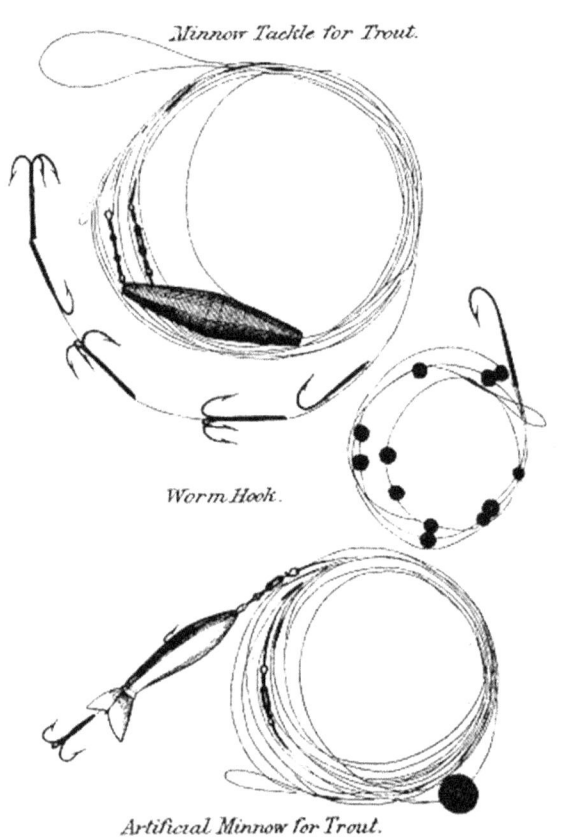

Plate 1.

Minnow Tackle for Trout.

Worm Hook.

Artificial Minnow for Trout.

BLACKER'S ANGLING.

BAIT FISHING.—THE RIVER THAMES.

After jumping over old "tower'd" Thames on our way to the south, we now return to him to wind up this little chapter on rivers; there cannot be a better river for the purposes of trolling, spinning, or bait fishing in general, than the Thames, there is not a town on its banks from Richmond to Oxford, that does not afford capital angling with the bait, and in many places large trout may be caught with the fly in the evening, these large trout are very delicious and grow fat on the quantities of minnows and gudgeons which they prey upon, and of which there are an inexhaustible supply. I have taken a few of them with large size blood red flies, brown flies, and large palmers of the like colours. The flies Nos. 4, 5, and 7, in the plates, are just the sort made a size or two smaller; Hampton Court, Sunbury, Weybridge, and Pentonhook, are likely places to rise a fish about seven in the evening, and early in the morning from six to eight. A light general rod with spare tops for fly fishing, about sixteen or seventeen feet long, with reel, and line of sixty yards, would be about the sort I would recommend, made of good hickory, or split cane; this sort of rod would suit any purpose, either for trolling, spinning, or for barbel fishing with the lob worm, &c.

Mr. Stoddart in his "Work on Angling" speaks very highly of worm and bait fishing in general.

And "Mr. Salter's Book," is a very good authority for trolling and spinning. The greater part of the fishermen and punt men on the Thames are capital hands at using the trolling and spinning tackle, so that the young angler who desires to become expert at this sort of fishing, can easily gain instruction from these civil men; they are also good barbel and trout fishers with the lob worm.

There are many good trout caught by spinning, and when bait fishing with the lob worm for barbel in places where they would rise and take the fly were they let alone, this is the cause of their being so scarce, as trout from half-a-pound and upwards will take the worm.

The Thames produces many kinds of fish—trout, perch, barbel, pike, roach, dace, carp, chub, gudgeons, minnows, eels, &c. As all these fish take the bait in general, I will here give the proper sorts for each, with the tackle to suit the purpose, and will show the angler which to use to his best advantage in every river he fishes in.

PERCH.

The Perch is a very handsome fish, and is best taken with the worm or live minnow, the larger size ones take the latter bait well and the smaller ones take the brandling and red worms best, using a No. 7 or 8 hook, and put on two worms at a time; use a small cork float, and as many shot on the line as will keep the bait steady about a foot from the bottom; use fine tackle in clear deep water, and keep as much out of their view as possible; the Paternoster is an excellent tackle for taking them, baited with live minnows in rapid waters near the sides of weirs, roving with a small live minnow, having a shot on the line of fine gut to keep it in mid water. If you know there are pike in the place, use fine gymp instead of gut, as these fish are taken in the same manner.

BARBEL.

The Barbel are strong fish, and require strong tackle to catch them, a No. 4 or 5 hook tied on stout single gut, and have a small bullet with a hole through it on your line, and a shot about a foot from the hook to be stationary, to prevent the bullet from running down on the bait; when you have a bite he draws the line through the bullet gently at first let him do so for a little, and then strike not too hard. The best bait for him is the lob worm well scoured.

Blacker's Art of Fly Making, &c.,

Plate 3.

Artificial Minnow for Jack.

Pike Spinning Tackle.

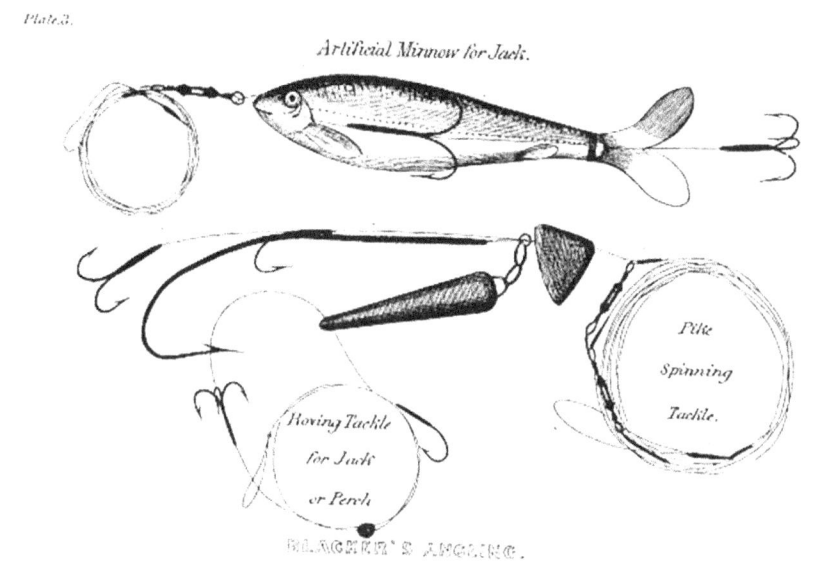

Roving Tackle for Jack or Perch

BLACKER'S ANGLING.

I consider this a famous plan for catching salmon, when they will not rise at the fly, in deep running streams. If you can find out where there is one lying drop it into the water above him and let it fall towards his nose, and he will be almost sure to take it. In low water you can throw the lob worm, if well scoured, on a gut casting line, like the fly, on a No. 6 hook; moving up the river, throwing it in before you, and allowing it to fall gently with the current till you feel a bite, raising your hand after allowing time, the same as if it had taken the fly; you may wade up the river at convenient places with your boots, try Cording's waterproofs, in the Strand.

There is good trout fishing after rains, with the running line, with shot attached; use gut hooks No. 7 or 8, and let the bait run with the stream gently, keeping the line taut, and when it stops rise your hand a little to free it, allowing it to move on again, and when you feel a bite wait a little till he takes it, and then strike gently, if a small fish pull him out, if a large one play him. The best places to throw in are at the sides of streams, in the smooth parts, in eddies, and where the current of the pool is breaking off at the foot into another stream, and when the flood is subsiding after rain, are the best times, using brandling worms and small lob worms. This was my favourite way of catching trout when a boy.

PIKE.

The Pike is a rough customer (if large) to come across, and the tackle which is required to catch him is as rough and as terrible as himself; he will take almost anything that is thrown to him if moved in the water he haunts. Roving with the minnow using a float, is, I think, the nicest way of fishing for him in deep places, but he is oftener taken by spinning, or trolling the gorge bait, tackle which is well known to every angler.

The pike take the larger double hook gaudy fly, in deep running places, beyond the weeds, when there is a stiff breeze blowing and small close rain falling, and at no other time will he look at a fly; it is useless to try unless in a rapid stream, which is an unusual place for him to haunt in general. Autumn is the best time for these fish. When you prepare the trolling bait for jack or pike, have a needle to draw the gymp through the bait, say a minnow, gudgeon, or dace, putting it in at the mouth of the fish and out near the root of the tail; sew up the mouth of the bait, and tie the tail part to the end of the hooks, which has been often explained before. Throw it in sideways into deep places, letting it sink a foot or two, and draw it in pretty quick towards you, and when the fish makes a run to take it, give him a little time; when your line begins to shiver and shake and he moves off, raise your hand and anchor the hook in him; if he is a small one whip him out of the water with your stiff and patent line at your feet, if a large one play him as you would a salmon, keep his head well up and draw him through the weeds if any and gaff him quickly.

The best rods to use for trolling are made of the toughest hickory, as the cane often gives way with a large fish; upright rings, and prepared silk and hair line, with reel to suit the rod, forty yards, if the place you angle in is not very broad, will be sufficient; and when fishing in a boat with a salmon rod, if there is a chance of pike fishing in lakes when the salmon will not take the fly, using the short top would be found stiff enough, that is, when you have not a trolling rod with you in the boat.

The large flexible minnow would be a capital bait for jack in lakes or deep rivers; and the glass minnow is also good. These fish rush at very bright imitations of the natural fish bait best, and a good size white trout would be a valuable little fish to throw for him—a large size dace is also good. These baits could be preserved in whiskey for weeks. They preserve fry and sprats in Scotland in this way for salmon or pike fishing. The old fishermen in the north say that "sprats" are the fry of the herring. I am persuaded that they would be excellent bait for salmon, pre-preserved so as to keep their brilliancy. The Paternoster Tackle cannot fail to suit the purpose of those who prefer angling in a punt for jack at the sides of large streams near the bank where there are alders or willows growing, overhanging the water, with a gravelly bottom. Nice plump bright minnows are the best, or large size gudgeons; the hooks No. 4 or 5, mounted on gymp.

Note.—The best trolling rods, spinning, and bait rods, with trolling tackle of the strongest sort; minnow tackle, gut hooks, gymp hooks, treble and double hooks, gorge and snap hooks, and every sort of the best hooks and tackle to suit trolling, spinning, and bait fishing, to be had at my shop, 54, Dean Street, Soho, London. Try my spinning trace, half twisted and half single salmon gut, mounted with swivels and large shot, for large trout or salmon.

ROACH.

The Roach is a handsome fish, and when taken of the size of half a pound or a pound, are not such bad eating as is said of them. They are very bony, it is true, but particularly wholesome. These fish do not thrive so well in ponds where they are exceedingly numerous, but in deep running rivers, with sandy and gravelly bottoms. They excel in both flavour and size. Let the place to angle for them be about four or five feet deep, plumb the depth, and allow your bait to be very near the bottom. The baits are paste, or gentles. When you begin, throw into the place you angle in some ground bait, to bring them together; keep your eye to the float, which should be a quill one, and the gut line with as many shot attached to it as will carry the float about a quarter the length of it out of the water, and strike smartly, but gently when you see it move downwards. They bite best in mild dark days. Work the paste between the hands (bread without wet), and when rather tough, mix a little vermilion with it, they like this best. Let the shot be about half a foot or so from the hook, which should be a No. 10 or 12, and where there are large ones, No. 8, tied on gut. When I was a little boy this sort of angling used to be my favourite amusement, with the running bait for trout after a flood.

DACE.

The Dace is a lively brisk little fish, and affords much amusement in catching him, particularly with very small flies, which he will rise at from May to October. They like the rapid streams, along the sides of them, and in the middle, they may be seen in shoals. The vicinity of Richmond is a very good place to go for a day's Dace fishing with the fly. They haunt the same places as the Roach, are taken with the same baits, and angled for near the bottom. Hooks No. 12 or 13.

CARP.

It is a very difficult matter to catch Carp with the bait, as they are most cunning fish to detect at once the deception, and swim away on the least sight of the rod or the shadow of the fisherman. The Carp haunt the deep parts of gently running streams, and those caught in rivers are the best; those that are very numerous in ponds are lean and soft in the flesh, and rather insipid. The best plan to angle for them would be with a very fine gut line, a No. 9 hook, baited with a couple of small red worms or two gentles, thrown into the water where they are, very cautiously, and keep well out of sight. Let the bait sink a short way from the surface, and draw it gently towards you, using at the same time a very long rod, rather stiff. Strike immediately they take the bait, gently, and play them as you would a trout on the fly.

CHUB.

The Chub is rather a handsome fish when in season, and those caught with the artificial fly in many parts of the Thames, are very brilliant and pretty to look at; but, unfortunately, they are full of very small bones, when cooked the roe is wholesome.

They haunt the deepest pools and rivers under shaded banks overhung with trees, the sides of weirs, and in ponds where a small spring runs in and out of them, with rather a rocky or gravelly bottom. Autumn is the best season for them, although I have caught them with the fly in the Thames in summer in good perfection, when fishing for trout. The way to angle for them would be to use a quill float, with a No. 8 hook, or larger, a gut line, and some shot about ten inches from the bait to sink the float, bait the hook with bread paste made red, and made tough in clean hands, put on a piece of it the size of a nut, throw in gently, and keep out of sight. Good cheese, well worked to make it tough, is also good. They will take gentles turned inside out on the hook one over the other, and when you have a bite strike rather quickly. They will also take grasshoppers, blue bottles, cadbait, and cockchafers; and with red or yellow flies, and black and brown palmers in the ordinary way of fishing for trout.

GUDGEONS AND MINNOWS.

These are very beautiful little fish, and most wholesome food; they are the best bait for perch, jack, and large trout, that can be, as I mentioned before. The way to angle for them is to have a couple of very small hooks tied on hair or fine gut, with a shot or two to carry the float off the bottom, say a small quill float, bait your hook with a very small red worm, or a piece of a brandling worm; they may be seen very numerous in the Thames, along the sides of streams, and in smooth running water with gravelly bottom; they afford nice amusement to the young angler, and when taken out of the water are remarkably handsome to look at.

BAITS.

To scour worms:—put them in clean damp moss, changing it in two or three days, place them between two layers of it, and choose those that are free from knots. The lob worms are found in gardens; brandlings and red worms are scoured with the lob worm in the same pot covered at top; those found in old tan yards are the best, and may be used without scouring. When you use the worms, dip them in cream, which will refresh their colour.

The cadis worm or cad bait is excellent for trout fishing, placed on the hook double, and cast gently with the wind into the stream, or dropped into the water beneath bushes that grow on the banks of pools where large fish lie, and are the most likely places. In rivers clearing off after floods in the summer they do well, and are also good for perch in deep running water. These cad worms produce many of the flies for the season after remaining during the cold weather at the bottom rolling about, and when the spring and summer appear they change into these beautiful insects; before the change takes place, during the winter, they form themselves a cover to protect them from the inroads of their enemies. Their instinct[8] prompts them to incase themselves like a snail in a piece of hollow reed, open at each end, and covered with small gravel and little shells, which they attach with a kind of glutinous substance to resist the force of the water; they creep on the bottom with six legs, and having their little house on their backs draw into it at pleasure, and settle amongst the stones like a piece of rotten branch or stick. The Trout and other fish feed upon them in the winter, when the winged insects are nowhere to be seen.

---

[8] **FOOTNOTE:** Given them by the Great Author of nature.

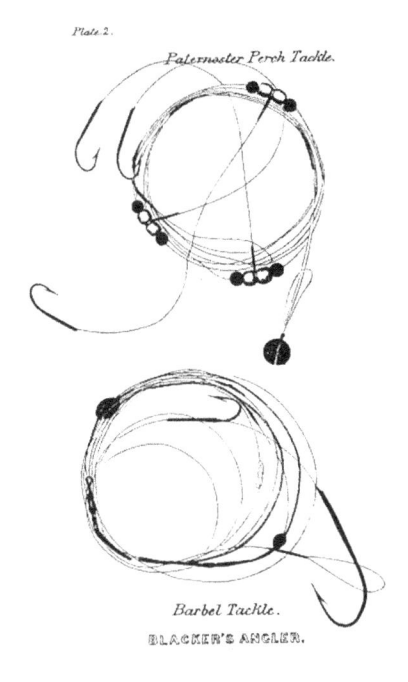

Showery windy days are generally best for fly fishing, blowing from the south, south-west, west, and north; there are but few fish take in east winds. When the wind blows warm in the beginning of the season it is good for bait fishing, and in autumn mild days are best. In days when there is no likelihood of constant rain after clear nights, and a nice grey cloud covers the sky, with a good cool breeze blowing to ripple the water, this is the time to rise the large trout, and which afford the best sport.

> "Full nature swarms with one wondrous mass
> Of animals, or atoms organized,
> Waiting the vital breath, when parent heaven
> Shall bid His spirit blow."
> Thomson.

William Blacker

THE ART OF DYEING FISHING COLOURS,
WHICH ARE
PIG'S HAIR, MOHAIR, FUR, & HACKLES, COMMONLY CALLED DUBBING.

The great advantage the fly fisher must derive from a knowledge of dyeing his colours and hackles is obvious. It affords amusement to the enthusiastic fisher to be acquainted with the various shades required for making his flies to suit the rivers, and the flies become valuable when made of good colours and hackles. Every hackle and colour that is used for making a salmon fly must be of the richest dye imaginable, that they may show brilliant and good to the fish's eye at the bottom of the water, and entice them to rise and take it at the top. The hackles must be taken from old cocks, both the neck and saddle ones, as they hold the dye best. Wool is not good for the fly, as it soaks the water, and is dull and heavy. Pig hair, that next the skin, with the stiff and coarse bristles picked and cleared away, and mohair, which is Spanish goat hair, a most beautiful brilliant substance for fly making when dyed well; white seal's fur, and furs of different kinds of a white colour. White hackles are best for yellows, oranges, gold colours, blues, greens, &c.; red hackles do best to dye claret, red, or fiery browns, olives, and cinnamon browns, &c., and black hackles for sooty olives, and tawny colours. When the angler sees a white old cock he should buy him to procure his hackles, or a black cock, a grey cock, and old red cocks of every hue, all of which are good for dyeing. These also must be washed in soap and hot water before being dyed, and the flue stripped off, tied in bunches (see the bunch of white hackles in the Plate of Feathers, ready for the dye) of proper sizes, and when about to be put into the dye-pot, wet them and the hair in hot water.

Provide a small crucible or earthen pot, glazed inside, with an earthen handle, to hold a quart of soft water, and before you put in your hackles or hair, wash them well, as I said before, in soap and hot water. The five principal colours to work upon are blue, red, yellow, brown, and black. From the combination of two or more of these may be produced every shade required, from the lightest to the darkest, so that it only requires some practice, to know the different ingredients to use, to become a Dyer of Fishing Colours.

TO DYE YELLOW.

I will begin with yellow, the most useful colour in general for the gentle craft. Put your crucible on a slow fire nearly full of water, or say half full, for the first trial. Take a tea cup, and into it put a table-spoonful of the best turmeric, pour over it some warm water, and stir it well with a clean piece of fire wood; when the water begins to simmer in the pot, put in the ingredient out of the cup, and stir it well with a piece of stick; have a second crucible, about half full of soft water, and boil it, into this put two table-spoonfuls of ground alum and one tea-spoonful of crystal of tartar, while these are boiling and perfectly dissolved, put into it your hackles or hair, and boil gently for an hour or half an hour; take off your pots and enter the hackles into the yellow dye out of the liquor into which you put the alum and tartar, and boil them very slowly for an hour, taking them out at intervals to see the shade you require; if too pale you must put more turmeric in, and if too heavy in shade the next trial, put in less, and do the same with all colours till you please your own eye. When they are the proper colour, take them out and wash them in soap and hot water. Draw them evenly through your fingers in the bunch, and let them dry, as this keeps them in shape.

There are three or four ways to dye yellow by changing the stuff. Fill your pots nearly full of soft water, and put into one the tartar and alum, and into the other two or three handfuls of yellow wood, which must be boiled slowly for three or four hours; when it is well boiled, strain off the liquor from the wood into a basin, and throw the wood away; put the dyeing liquor into the pot again, and when boiling take out the hackles from the mordant of tartar and alum and put them into the yellow dye, let them boil gently for some time till the yellow colour has entered the hackles or hair, then take them out and wash them in soap and water, straighten them between the fingers, and let them dry; take them in the right hand and strike them on the fore-finger of the left till they are quite dry.

By boiling two handfuls of fustic and a table-spoonful of turmeric together, and repeating the above process, there will be produced a golden yellow, which is very good for fly making. There must not be too much alum used, neither must the ingredients be boiled too long. Persian berries, bruised and boiled slowly, with a spoonful of turmeric, produces a good yellow; and an ingredient called weld, boiled as before, and adding the alum, is a good dye for yellow,—indeed, the weld is the best dye, if care is taken with it.

TO DYE BROWN.

Put into your dye pot about two handfuls of walnut rinds, or as much as it will hold nicely to boil; simmer this slowly over the fire for three or four hours, and add a little water to it as it boils away. When all the juice of the dye is taken out of the rinds, strain the liquor off, put it into the basin, and throw away the rinds; you take two handfuls more and boil them in the same way, and add the stuff together in the pot; the rinds being thrown away, put your hackles, &c., previously washed, into the dye, and simmer them on the fire for four or five hours, till you have the proper colour struck on the hackles. The alum and tartar need not be added to this dye.

Take out the feathers and wash them well; the walnut roots cut small, dye in the same way.

TO DYE A YELLOW BROWN.

The Saunders' Wood, brought from the Indies, and sold in powder or ground mixed with sumach is good, it takes long to boil, adding the alum.

A Cinnamon Brown or Fiery Brown may be struck on the hackles or colours (pig hair or mohair) by first dyeing them yellow, the same as explained in the yellow dye; put the hackles, previously dyed yellow, into the liquor of walnut rinds, and simmer them over the fire slowly for three or four hours, and leave them in all night, if a dark fiery brown is required; the less of the rinds produce cinnamon or yellow brown, the roots and rinds of the walnut are the best for the various shades; the rind of the alder dyed with alum and tartar is also good.

TO DYE BLUE.

Fill your crucible three parts full of soft water, and put it on a slow fire, at the same time put in your blue ingredients, previously prepared, (this is done by dissolving the powdered blue in oil of vitriol and water in a stopper bottle for twenty-four hours). If there is a very light shade of blue required, put in a couple of table-spoonfuls of the blue ingredient, and add to it as the shade may be varied at will according to the quantity of the stuff; boil the hackles in tartar and alum, say a table-spoonful of each, or rather less of the tartar, simmer it on the fire for two or three hours according to the process mentioned before; and when the proper colour is produced take out the hackles, hair, or fur, and wash them well in soap and hot water.

There is a paste blue prepared at the dry-salters all ready for the dye pot, take a table-spoonful of it and stir it well up in your pot nearly full of soft water, and boil it gently for about an hour (or less), then put in your hackles or hair, previously washed and wet going in, boil for two hours very slowly and wash off the dye; any shade of blue may be had in a very short time by this process; there are two or three dry-salters in Long Acre where this paste blue is sold, and any of the other ingredients may be purchased at their shops, or at chymists.

TO DYE RED.

Prepare your dye pot by nearly filling it with soft water; and keep it at a scalding heat when the dye stuff is put in, as it must not boil, if it is allowed to boil it becomes dull in colour; put into the dye pot a handful of finest grape madder, and simmer it slowly over the fire, stir well, and prepare the hackles or hair in the alum and red tartar liquor; after having boiled an hour slowly, take out a bunch and look at them between your eyes and the sun or light to see how they take the dye, if too pale there must be more madder added, and allow them to remain in the dye all night, simmer them slowly, next day take them out, rinse and wash them well, and allow them to dry in the air; mix a table-spoonful of cochineal with the madder.

TO DYE ORANGE.

When orange is desired take a handful of best madder and mix it with a spoonful of cochineal, boil it for an hour or two, add too a little ground red wood which requires more boiling than the madder itself; dye your hackles or stuff yellow first, and dip them into the red dye a short time, take them out and look at the shade you have; if too light allow them to remain in longer, and you will have darker shades of colour, put a little red tartar and ground alum into the dye to assist the red wood to strike on the materials, take them out and wash them in soap and hot water, and afterwards rinse them in urine which gives a lustre and softness to the stuff.

TO DYE PURPLE OR VIOLET.

First dye the hackles or stuffs blue, and lay them to dry; then, fill the dye-pot more than half with soft water, and in the other pot prepare the tartar and alum, dip your hackles into this for a little while, and lay them on the table till you prepare the red dye; bruise a couple of table-spoonfuls of cochineal, and put them into the pot of hot soft water, boil for an hour, and put in the blue hackles, and allow them to simmer over the fire very slowly to keep them from burning; when you have the proper shade, take them out and wash them well.

TO DYE CRIMSON.

Boil your hackles or hair in a tea-spoonful of alum, and nearly as much pure tartar, for an hour; bruise two table-spoonfuls of cochineal, and boil them in your clean water; take out the hackles from the alum-water, and put them into the cochineal liquor, and boil for two or three hours slowly or less, according to the shade you require; then take out the feathers and wash them well, and you will have the color desired.

TO DYE SCARLET.

Boil your hackles, &c., in a little crystal of tartar; procure two tablespoonfuls of cochineal, bruise them a little, and boil them gently over the fire for an hour or two; take the hackles you have just boiled in the tartar, and put them into the dye-pot, and simmer them slowly for some time, say half an hour; then take your "spirits of grain,"[9] and put into the dye-pot a tea-spoonful or a little more; take them out occasionally, and look at them between your eyes and the light, and when the right shade is obtained, rinse them and dry.

If you are in a hurry for scarlet, you may drop the particles of block-tin into aqua-fortis till they are dissolved, and add a little to the scarlet dye; the other is best, as it gives a more brilliant shade;—boil slow.

If the extract of bismuth is added to the red liquor of the cochineal in a small quantity, it will change it to a purple or violet colour.

CRIMSON RED IN GRAIN.

Boil your hackles or hair in a quarter of an ounce of alum, and the same quantity of pure tartar, an hour gently; wash them out of this, fill your dye-pot with clean water, or as much as will conveniently boil; put in an ounce of well-powdered dye stuff they call "grain," with one drachm of red arsenic, and one spoonful of burnt wine lees, this gives a lustre; wash and rinse well after boiling a short time, and the colour is good.

---

[9] **FOOTNOTES:** Spirits of grain for scarlet,—a quarter pint of spirits of nitre, a quarter of an ounce of ammoniac, add half water in a bottle, and drop into it half an ounce of block-tin in grains till dissolved.

TO DYE GREEN DRAKE, FEATHERS AND FUR.

Boil your hackles, mohair, or fur, in alum and tartar, a quarter of an ounce of each; rinse them well, and put them into the dye-pot, with an ounce of savory, and as much green-wood as the pot will contain; (it is best to boil off the savory and green-wood first, throw away the wood, and boil the feathers in the liquor;) boil gently, and look at the feathers occasionally to see if they are the right shade, these give the natural shades of yellow green. The quantity of tartar and alum, and of dye-stuff is given in this dye; and the preceding which will show what must be used in all shades of colour, according to the quality or your own taste.

TO DYE CLARET.

Boil two handfuls of red-wood, or ground Brazil-wood, for an hour, with a handful of log-wood; then take a table-spoonful of oil of vitriol, and put it into half a tea cup of cold water; and when the dye-pot is a little cold, add it to the liquor, stir it, and put it on with the hackles or hair, and boil it gently for two hours; take out your material, and put it into cold water; add to the dye it comes out of a little copperas, and a small quantity of pearlashes, about the size of a nut of copperas, and a quarter that size of the ashes; put in your hackles or material again, and when the proper shade is obtained, rinse and wash well, and finish in urine, which brightens them, and your colour is good.

ANOTHER WAY TO DYE CLARET.

Take a handful of nut galls and bruise them, put them into the crucible and boil them half an hour, add to the dye a table-spoonful of oil of vitriol in half a cup of water, put in the hackles and boil two hours; then add to the liquor a little pearl ashes, and a piece of copperas the size of a nut, boil gently for two hours or as long as required to suit the taste of the dyer, rinse and wash them well, the ashes need not be used in this dye, but if used a very small quantity will suffice.

Another way:—boil red wood powdered for two hours (two handfuls), and then put the hackles in, boil an hour longer, let the liquor cool, and put into a tea cup half full of water nearly a table-spoonful of aquafortis and pour it into the dye, stir well occasionally and keep the hackles down, boil for two hours more and rinse off, finish in a little urine. If a very dark claret is required lay them in to boil for a day and night with a scalding heat.

TO DYE BLACK.

Boil two good handfuls of log-wood with a little sumach and elder bark for an hour, put in the stuff or hackles (boil very gently), bruise a piece of copperas about the size of two Spanish nuts, put it in with a little argil and soda; take out the hackles and hold them in the open air a little, then put them in again and leave them all night gently heated, wash the dye well out of them and your black will be fine. The argil and soda soften the dye stuff of the copperas, but a small quantity must be put in.

TO DYE GREENS OF VARIOUS SHADES.

The greatest nicety of all is in finding the exact quantity of ingredients to put in, so as to prevent the dye stuff from injuring the fibres of the hackles, &c.; for the light shades add the smallest quantity, and augment it by degrees. Dye the hackles a very light shade of blue first, in prepared indigo,[10] as I said before, take a spoonful and put it into the dye

---

[10] **FOOTNOTE:** Half a tea cupful of water, and the same quantity of oil of vitriol, put into a bottle, the indigo to remain in twenty-four hours to dissolve.

pot and boil it softly for half an hour. Add a very small quantity of alum and tartar to the dye, put in your hackles, and boil for a short time; add to the dye a table-spoonful of the best turmeric, savoy, or green wood, a little of each would do best, boil slowly for an hour, take out the hackles, rinse them, and you will have a green: you may have any shade of green by dyeing the blues darker or lighter, and putting in more yellowing stuff and less blue when light yellow greens are required, boil gently, and look at the hackles often to see that they have taken the shade you want.

TO DYE LAVENDER OR SLATE DUN, &c.

Boil ground logwood with bruised nut galls and a small quantity of copperas, according to judgment: you may have a pigeon dun, lead colour, light, or dark dun. The ingredients must be used in small quantities, according to taste. You may have raven grey, or duns of various shades, by boiling with the logwood a small quantity of alum and copperas.

BLUES.

Dissolve some indigo in oil of vitriol for twenty-four hours, put a couple of spoonfuls in your pot, add a little crystal of tartar, put in your hackles and boil, or at least keep them at a scalding heat, or the vitriol will burn the feathers, furs, &c., take them out, rinse them well, and the colour will be lasting.

If to the above liquor some fustic chips, well boiled by themselves, and the juice added, you may then have any shade of the best green.

A SILVER GREY.

Boil some fenugreek and a little alum half an hour, put in the white hackles, &c., and add a little pearlash and Brazil-wood, boil them gently an hour, rinse them, and your colour will be lasting.

A COFFEE OR CHESNUT.

Boil the hackles, &c., that have been previously dyed brown, in some nut gall, sumach, and alder bark, then add a small quantity of green copperas to the liquor, allow it to remain a day and a night in water that you can bear the hand in, and all the stuff will enter the materials.

TO DYE OLIVES AND A MIXTURE OF COLOURS.

Olives are dyed from blue, red, and brown, of every shade, according to fancy.

From yellow, blue, and brown, are made olives of all kinds.

From brown, blue, and black, brown and green olives are made.

From red, yellow, and brown, are produced orange, gold colour, marigold, cinnamon, &c.

See Haigh's Dyer's Assistant of Woollen Goods, for larger quantities.

A CONCISE WAY OF DYEING COLOURS.

I will now add the way to dye the colours, for pighair, mohair, hackles, &c., in a concise and summary manner, to avoid giving trouble in too many words, and the quantities of ingredients I have given before, which would be superfluous to mention over so often, and which the dyer must know by this time. The great art is in knowing the quantities that each dye requires to obtain the exact colour, and this may be known by a close observation to the rules I have given.

Fustic and alum water will dye yellow, the hackles dipped three times in fresh stuff. Weld, turmeric, and fenugreek, will give a yellow, boiled in alum water, and the hackles dipped often, till they are the proper colour.

These may be dyed without tartar at pleasure.

Brazil-wood, boiled till you have a strong decoction, strain off the juice, then add alum water, boil the hackles in it slowly for a day or two, and it will produce good reds. If the colour of the Brazil-wood be very strong, there may be reds obtained in an hour's boiling. This is a wood which is of a hard nature, and it is difficult to extract the colour from it, although a good dye.

A claret may be produced from Brazil-wood mixed with red archil, and boiled in the usual manner, dipped in potash liquor, or brilla will act in the same way to strike the colour; use hard water.

A fiery brown may be made from fustic and turmeric boiled together with alum and a little crystal of tartar, (soft water for this dye), and then dip in liquor of potash.

A cinnamon brown may be made with a little madder, or stone crottle, boiled with alum and tartar, with a little turmeric to finish it.

A good blue may be had by boiling the hackles with alum water, and add a spoonful of the liquid blue; this is done by putting some oil of vitriol into a bottle with a little water, and then the indigo, powdered, which will dissolve in twenty-four hours, and be ready for use. (I have mentioned this twice before, as I am very particular.)

For a purple, dye blue first, then add the red dye, and dip it in potash; when the hackles, &c., are left long in the red, it is more of a wine purple.

To have a good green, dye blue first, then boil in turmeric and fustic bark, with alum and tartar, as usual. You may have any shade of green by noticing the process in the dye pot.

To dye an orange, first make it a turkey red with Brazil-wood and alum water, then finish with turmeric and fustic till the colour pleases you.

To dye a golden olive, boil sumach and turmeric with alum water, add a little potash and copperas, and finish with new turmeric and a little potash.

Green olive may be made with a little more copperas and verdigris.

Sooty olive is made by adding to the first a little alder or oak bark, and finishing with turmeric and alum water.

An amber may be made with red, and finished with yellow dye; the first with stone crottle or madder, and finish with turmeric bark; the yellow with alum water. All fishing colours should be dyed yellow first with alum and crystal of tartar, but claret.

Claret may be made from Brazil-wood, barked first in alum water, adding new Brazil three or four times fresh to the liquor, and simmer slowly for a day or two.

A fiery brown may be made from lima or peth-wood, barked with turmeric and alum water.

A golden yellow may be had from citrine bark, boiled in new stuff three times slowly, bark with alum, and dip in potash or brilla.

All blues may be dipped in potash, to sadden the colour.

A crottle or red orange, boil madder and stone crottle together, and bark with alum water; the madder will do if the crottle cannot be had. The crottle grows on stones in rocky places, like red moss.

An orange may be had by dyeing yellow in strong liquid three times fresh; bark with alum, and dip in potash.

A Green Drake may be made by dyeing a good yellow first, and adding a few drops of the blue decoction from the bottle of prepared blue dye, this comes to the green drake colour; add a little copperas to make a green dark or light, as you please.

A golden olive may be made by dyeing brown red hackles in fustic and a little copperas, and dipped in potashes, finished in turmeric and alum; you will have a sooty olive by adding but very little of the turmeric root.

A sooty olive may be made by dyeing black hackles in yellow first with alum water, add fresh yellow stuff three times to the dye pot, and dip them in potashes.

A wine purple may be made from light dyed blue hackles, put them in the red dye of madder, Brazil, or cochineal, and dip them twice in potashes.

Liver-coloured hackles may be had from brown red hackles, barked with alum, and boiled in Brazil-wood juice, dipped in liquor of potash.

A bright olive may be made from fustic and oak bark, adding a little turmeric and alum water.

A fiery cinnamon may be had from yellow dye, Brazil juice, and madder mixed, boil these well, and add a little turmeric with alum.

A golden crottle may be made from stone crottle and yellow dyes with turmeric and alum water. The stone crottle is best for all golden colours, but as it may not be easily got at, use madder instead; golden orange may be had from the above, adding a little potashes, and boil very slowly.

A pea green may be had by dyeing yellow first, and add a few drops out of the blue dye bottle, till it comes to the shade, it may be darkened to a leek or bottle green.

A stone blue,—bark the hackle with alum, and add to the alum water as much of the prepared dye out of the bottle as will make it dark enough, this may be easily seen from the appearance of the liquor in the dye pot.

A Prussian blue is done in the same way, keeping out the indigo, and adding the Prussian blue.

Dip a red into potashes and you have a light wine purple; blue and red dye is best.

Dip a good yellow in potashes, well boiled and stir, and you will have an orange. A little tartar is good for all colours but black.

Sumach, logwood, iron liquor, and copperas, will form a black. Boil a small quantity of copperas with logwood, and it will dye gut properly.

A tawny cinnamon may be dyed from stone crottle or madder, mixed with turmeric, alum, and a little tartar, these must be gently boiled in fresh stuff, adding a little copperas.

THE MATERIALS NECESSARY FOR ARTIFICIAL FLY MAKING.

The necessary articles used for fly making in general are as follows: Those feathers that are of a most gaudy hue are best for the wings of salmon flies, which are golden pheasant feathers, cock of the rock, the crest of the Hymalaya pheasant, the blue and yellow macaw, the scarlet macaw, red macaw, green parrot's feathers, particularly the Amazon parrot tail, the scarlet Ibis, blue king fishers, and chattern, the splendid Trogan, the Argus pheasant, the bustard, red parrot, and the Bird of Paradise; the wood-duck feathers (try the cock of the north feathers, black hackle, white body, and gold); the jungle cock; the spotted turkey, brown, light, and dark feathers; brown mallard, or wild drake; teal feathers; heron feather, black and blue; glede or kite tail feathers; grey mallard, widgeon, and shovel duck; various dyed and natural cock hackles; grouse hackles; guinea hen hackles, the rump and back feathers; silver pheasant, cock and hen bird tail, wings, and body feathers; yellow toucan feathers; blue jay feathers, and the wings of the jay for trout flies; peacock feathers, off wings, tail, and body; black ostrich feathers, and the white ostrich for dyeing all colours for the heads of flies, &c., with floss silk of every shade; gold and silver twist, and plate of different sizes; pighair, mohair, furs, &c.

The materials for small trout flies are, mohair, furs of every colour, water rat, fitch, squirrel, mole's fur, hare's ears and neck furs, mouse and common rat fur, martin's fur, sable fur, black spaniel's hair off the ear, black bear's hair for tailing the drake, and all white furs dyed of various shades, such as yellow, yellow-green, gold, orange, cinnamon, light duns, &c.; starling wings, grouse feathers, snipe wings, woodcock wings, thrush and blackbird's wings, fieldfare wings, wren tails, tomtit tails, bunton lark wing, skylark wings, sparrow wings, landrail wings, water-hen wings, water-rail wings, partridge tails and hackle feathers, brown hen wings, tail, and body feathers, dun hen wings, &c.; dun cock hackles, dun hen hackles, dottril wings and hackles, and all dun, brown, and grey feathers that can be found on every bird that flies are useful for imitating the natural insects; tying silks of every shade, yellow and orange being the favorites; hooks of sizes, and silk-worm gut.

And now to wind up the line. I humbly beg to say that if I have deceived the friends of the rod in anything, they have a right to be indifferent with my profession of friendship, and ought to retain a sensibility of my misfortune; my conscience is clear it is not so, for I know that I would deceive myself were I to think that I could do without my admirable friends of the angle—without me they could do—but I value their worth, as in hope I rest, although they say "hope told a flattering tale." I am not deceived by flattery, be it far from us; I dislike deceit. I have hid nothing; I have done my endeavours in this book to show the youths of the angle, as well as the great fly fishers, all I know about the matter so far, and as the Chinamen say, that "time and industry convert a mulberry leaf into a silk shawl," so perseverance will be the means of the fly maker's success, if he allows himself an opportunity of accomplishing that which he requires to know and to perform, and at the same time neglect not to prepare for the "coming struggle," it will be his own fault if he does not become a skilful angler, &c. I will therefore consider myself highly honoured if the young gentlemen of England, Ireland, Scotland, and Wales, appreciate my labour, and to be enabled, by the natural genius they possess, descending from Him who visited us through the "Orient" from on high to enlighten our understandings in every good, to find out the information they desire in the perusal of these pages.

FINIS.

Also from Benediction Books …
Wandering Between Two Worlds: Essays on Faith and Art
Anita Mathias
Benediction Books, 2007
152 pages
ISBN: 0955373700

Available from www.amazon.com, www.amazon.co.uk

In these wide-ranging lyrical essays, Anita Mathias writes, in lush, lovely prose, of her naughty Catholic childhood in Jamshedpur, India; her large, eccentric family in Mangalore, a sea-coast town converted by the Portuguese in the sixteenth century; her rebellion and atheism as a teenager in her Himalayan boarding school, run by German missionary nuns, St. Mary's Convent, Nainital; and her abrupt religious conversion after which she entered Mother Teresa's convent in Calcutta as a novice. Later rich, elegant essays explore the dualities of her life as a writer, mother, and Christian in the United States-- Domesticity and Art, Writing and Prayer, and the experience of being "an alien and stranger" as an immigrant in America, sensing the need for roots.

About the Author

Anita Mathias is the author of *Wandering Between Two Worlds: Essays on Faith and Art*. She has a B.A. and M.A. in English from Somerville College, Oxford University, and an M.A. in Creative Writing from the Ohio State University, USA. Anita won a National Endowment of the Arts fellowship in Creative Nonfiction in 1997. She lives in Oxford, England with her husband, Roy, and her daughters, Zoe and Irene.

Visit Anita at
 http://www.anitamathias.com, and
Anita's blog Dreaming Beneath the Spires at:
 http://theoxfordchristian.blogspot.com, and
Anita's Read Through the Bible blog at:
 http://readthroughthebiblewithanita.blogspot.com/

The Church That Had Too Much
Anita Mathias
Benediction Books, 2010
52 pages
ISBN: 9781849026567

Available from www.amazon.com, www.amazon.co.uk

The Church That Had Too Much was very well-intentioned. She wanted to love God, she wanted to love people, but she was both hampered by her muchness and the abundance of her possessions, and beset by ambition, power struggles and snobbery. Read about the surprising way The Church That Had Too Much began to resolve her problems in this deceptively simple and enchanting fable.

About the Author

Anita Mathias is the author of *Wandering Between Two Worlds: Essays on Faith and Art*. She has a B.A. and M.A. in English from Somerville College, Oxford University, and an M.A. in Creative Writing from the Ohio State University, USA. Anita won a National Endowment of the Arts fellowship in Creative Nonfiction in 1997. She lives in Oxford, England with her husband, Roy, and her daughters, Zoe and Irene.

Visit Anita at
    http://www.anitamathias.com, and
Anita's blog Dreaming Beneath the Spires at:
    http://theoxfordchristian.blogspot.com, and
Anita's Read Through the Bible blog at:
    http://readthroughthebiblewithanita.blogspot.com/